MY LIFE
AND
PROPHECIES

Jeane Dixon

MY LIFE
AND
PROPHECIES

Her own story
as told to Rene Noorbergen

WILLIAM MORROW AND COMPANY, INC.
NEW YORK

To my devoted and understanding husband,
James Lamb Dixon . . .
and to my beloved mother and father, now in Heaven
yet ever with me,
this book is lovingly dedicated.

JEANE

A WORD OF GRATITUDE

My sincere appreciation to my good and valued friends,
William H. Graham, Adele Fletcher,
Judie Noorbergen, and Gertrude Parker.

Contents

AUTHOR'S NOTE

The purpose of this book is to show that as God spoke through the prophets so does He convey a message through each one of us. And that message is that each one of us has an individual purpose to fulfill in His Divine Plan.

Prologue

Writing a book is one thing; writing about Jeane Dixon is something else again. When she first asked me to help her write this book, I wondered how to approach the subject with true objectivity. Her predictions have informed presidents, warned politicians, baffled the skeptics, but also scared people out of their wits. To her, however, it is all very simple.

"Each of us has a talent that functions as a primary channel of communication between the Higher Power and ourself," she says. "I believe that a like spirit that worked through the Biblical prophets Isaiah and John the Baptist works through some of us. It is a reactivation of that similar power that has given me the inspiration for my revelations."

Truth or fiction? Many will never be able to make up their minds about her unless they are faced with the facts and examine them in the quiet of their own rooms.

Let's examine some of these facts and start from there.

In her late forties, a successful real estate broker, she has no reason to want to seek the limelight of publicity, for her life has been fulfilling enough ever since her psychic gift came to the surface. Ambassadors, statesmen, presidents, businessmen all seek her advice, and many a foreign dignitary prefers to have an appointment with Jeane Dixon instead of a private reception at the White House. Her reputation has reached far beyond our shores.

She has, however, remained humble through it all. She continues to turn down many offers for commercial appearances from major television networks; she returns all letters addressed to her in which fortune seekers ask advice purely for monetary reasons, spiking their requests with money. Her friends will vouch for her, and even her enemies must praise her for her sincerity.

To me, as a journalist, a story is only that until the facts become so realistic that they can stand by themselves. At that point reality takes over and the story becomes a "case history." Such is the case with the "Jeane Dixon story."

The questions "who" and "what" is Jeane Dixon are not easy to answer. One thing is sure—she is not an unusual phenomenon. There have been prophets since the beginning of time. Biblical prophets like Isaiah, Daniel, John the Baptist, Ezekiel, all had a message for their time and ours. Modern-day psychics have *their* place in history and seem to have filled a vacuum created by man's insecurity and growing uncertainty. Jeane Dixon feels her place is right here in the twentieth century, and her message is one directed at twentieth-century humanity.

Many experts vouch for her psychic ability.

One of the world's foremost psychic researchers, Dr. F. Regis Riesenman, tested thousands of people before and after he became interested in Jeane Dixon in 1959, and has come to the conclusion that *everyone* is psychic, without realizing it. *He is convinced that psychic sense was much more developed in primitive times when man had to fight for his existence.* "If man had not been able to sense danger around every corner," he stressed, "he would never have been able to survive the hostile jungle." This harmonizes with what Prof. Alfred M. Rehwinkel says in his book *The Flood.* In it he states, "When sin came into the world, *human intellect suffered as did the rest of his faculties.* But even after sin had come into the world, man remained a superior being, and the first race was decidedly a superior one."

How superior we will probably never know, but if there was really any relationship between mental ability and physical size, then it might be well to reexamine some scientific finds made in the early 1950's.

Roland T. Bird, of the American Museum of Natural History, reported finding giant petrified human footprints in the Paluxy River bed in Glen Rose, Texas. The prints would not have been so surprising if it had not been for the fact that they were seventeen inches long. Bird called them "the strangest things I ever found." A government trapper, Ellis Wright, reported a similar find in the same area. He stated that he had found no less than thirteen footprints, all petrified, and each one of them measured twenty-two inches in length and ten inches in width. Other tracks, possibly made by a member of the same race, were found in White Sands, New Mexico. The size of the tracks indicates that the "owner" must have weighed about five hundred pounds and have been ten to twelve feet in height!

What happened to these people? Why did this race disappear from the face of the earth? What is their secret? Something terrible must have happened in those days to explain the strange mysteries of the thousands of frozen dinosaurs and mammoths in the Gobi Desert and isolated sections of Siberia. What happened that was responsible for the fate of the tropical forests that are now covered by desert sands?

Acceptance of the Biblical account of the Deluge is one of the most reasonable ways to explain it. According to this account of the tragedy, the earth was much more fertile before the flood than it is today. Man and beast had access to all the nourishment necessary to grow to enormous proportions, and the absence of disease and inbreeding no doubt helped to keep the race in those proportions. Today, however, we have to go down into the ocean depths to find the largest living mammals—possibly because when the waters of the Deluge subsided, a large share of the fertile soil washed down into the basins that later became our oceans. Geologists such as Dr. George McCready Price hold this to be more than just a theory. One of the largest sea mammals, the whale, survived, while undernourished man, fighting for existence in a now hostile environment, underwent a process of devolution.

Can it be that the so-called "sixth sense" is an original sense that became dormant over the long centuries of human devolution together with a decrease in man's physical size? Can it be that the psychic ability of persons like Jeane Dixon is a restoration of something God endowed mankind with at the time of creation?

Dr. Riesenman says that most people have an ESP ability of between 3 and 7 percent. "But only three percent of these," he says, "are truly psychic." Of the remaining 97 percent he says that those cases are attributable to a subconscious evaluation of an emotion of some sort. Seventy percent of that group he dismisses as fraud or trickery.

Jeane Dixon's ESP ability, however, is for real and has been rated by him at between 90 and 97 percent!

While most responsible research scientists feel that psychic phenomena are transmitted from man to man, or from superior beings to man, on a frequency so far out of the known spectrum that it is impossible to detect, Cleve Backster, head of the Backster Research Foundation in New York, has discovered what appears to be the actual signal!

He has detected a method of communication that seems to connect all creation. He calls the signals the "first established evidence of primary communication."

Using a plant, hooked up to the sensing elements of a polygraph, commonly known as a lie detector, *he has sensed and recorded a form of actual communication between plant and animal life on a primary level.*

Backster's discovery indicates that primary perception exists down to the single cell level.

In an interview we had with him in regard to this discovery, Backster suggested that this revolutionary discovery is only the first step to an ultimate understanding of creation.

"I can't tell you what kind of signal it is that we have discovered," Backster admitted to us, *"but I do know what it is not.* It is not within the different known frequencies such as AM, FM, or any other form of signal which we can shield by ordinary means. We have tried to block the signal emanating from plants under stress or brine shrimp at the moment of death by the use of a Faraday screen and even lead containers, but the signals keep coming. I am sure that both Jeane Dixon and I have tapped into the frequency used by the Universal Intelligence although for different reasons.

"I do not doubt that this means of communication has always existed. We have blocked our extrasensory perception through our prejudices. We tell ourselves and science and our environment tell us that an extra sense is nonsense, yet put a man under hypnosis and give him a posthypnotic suggestion to ignore his prejudices and be open to extrasensory communication, and I'm sure he will receive more than he ever thought possible.

"Jeane Dixon's mind is open. She seems to have full access to a faculty which once was used quite extensively but has practically disappeared into the background through nonusage."

Jeane Dixon, while heartily endorsing this scientific foundation for her gift, nevertheless holds that it is only God's spirit, working through her, that is responsible for her visions and prophecies. Deeply religious, her faith in God is unshakable. During moments of discouragement, it's the Biblical foundation for her "gift of prophecy" that makes her push ahead the way "God wants it," as she says.

The Bible is filled with specific tests and requirements a prophet has to be able to meet before he or she can be called "a prophet of the Most High." It might be well to list them. They are interesting enough to be seriously considered.

1. *Can uninspired men of the world foretell the future?*
"Daniel answered before the king, and said, The secret which
the king hath demanded can neither wise men, enchanters,
magicians, nor soothsayers show unto the king." Daniel 2:27,
revised version.

2. *What belongs to God and what belongs to us?*
"The secret things belong unto the Lord our God: but those
things which are revealed belong unto us and to our children
forever." Deuteronomy 29:29.

3. *By what means did God deliver and preserve ancient
Israel?*
"By a prophet the Lord brought Israel out of Egypt, and by
a prophet was he preserved." Hosea 12:13.

4. *How does the Lord reveal Himself to His prophets?*
"If there be a prophet among you, I the Lord will make Myself
known unto him in a vision, and will speak unto him in a
dream." Numbers 12:6.

5. *Under what influence did the prophets of old speak?*
"For the prophecy came not in old time by the will of man:
but holy men of God spake as they were moved by the Holy
Ghost." 2 Peter 1:21.

6. *What Spirit was in God's prophets inspiring their
messages?*
"Of which salvation the prophets have inquired and
searched diligently, who prophesied of the grace that should
come unto you: searching what, or what manner of time the
Spirit of Christ which was in them did signify, when it testified beforehand the sufferings of Christ, and the glory that
should follow." 1 Peter 1:10, 11.

7. *How were the Lord's words to the prophets preserved?*
"Daniel had a dream and visions of his head upon his bed:
then he wrote the dream and told the sum of the matters."
Daniel 7:1. (See also Jeremiah 51:60; Revelation 1:11.)

8. *By what means has God generally made known His will
to man?*
"I have also spoken by the prophets, and I have multiplied

visions, and used similitudes, by the ministry of the prophets."
Hosea 12:10. (See also Hebrews 1:1, 2.)

9. *Who did Daniel say could reveal secrets?*
"But there is a God in heaven that revealeth secrets and
maketh known to the king Nebuchadnezzar what shall be in
the latter days." Daniel 2:28.

10. *How fully and to whom does God reveal His purposes?*
"Surely the Lord God will do nothing, but He revealeth His
secret unto His servants the prophets." Amos 3:7.

11. *Did God at any time bestow the gift of prophecy upon
women?*
"So . . . the priest . . . went unto Huldah the prophetess,
the wife of Shallum . . . and . . . communed with her. And
she said unto them, Thus saith the Lord God of Israel, Tell
the man that sent you to me." 2 Kings 22:14, 15.

Note: Commenting on 2 Kings 22:14, Joseph Priestley
remarks concerning Huldah: "It pleased God to distinguish
several women with the spirit of prophecy as well as other
great attainments, to show that, in his sight, and especially
in things of a spiritual nature, there is no essential preem-
inence in the male sex." *Notes on All the Books of Scripture,*
vol. 2, page 40.

12. *What test should be applied in determining the validity
of a person's claim to be a prophet?*
"If there arise among you a prophet, or a dreamer of dreams,
and giveth thee a sign or a wonder, and the sign or the wonder
come to pass, whereof he spake unto thee, saying, Let us go
after other gods, which thou hast not known, and let us serve
them; thou shalt not hearken unto the words of that prophet,
or that dreamer of dreams; for the Lord your God proveth
you, to know whether ye love the Lord your God with all
your heart and with all your soul. Ye shall walk after the
Lord your God, and fear Him, and keep His commandments,
and obey His voice, and ye shall serve Him, and cleave unto
Him." Deuteronomy 13:1-4.

13. *What rule did Christ give for distinguishing between true and false prophets?*
"By their fruits ye shall know them." Matthew 7:20.

14. *Are prophets called to minister to the church primarily or to non-Christians?*
"He that prophesieth edifieth the church." 1 Corinthians 14:4.

15. *To what fact about Jesus Christ does "the Spirit of God" bear witness?*
"Hereby know ye the Spirit of God: Every spirit that confesseth that Jesus Christ is come in the flesh is of God." 1 John 4:2. (See also verses 1, 3.)

Note: A true prophet's teaching will attest to the basic fact of Christ's incarnation and vicarious death, His resurrection, and His second advent.

16. *What attitude toward the gift of prophecy is recommended?*
"Despise not prophesyings. Prove all things, hold fast that which is good." 1 Thessalonians 5:20, 21.

17. *What were some of the gifts Christ gave to His church?*
"When He ascended up on high, He led captivity captive, and gave gifts unto men . . . And he gave some, apostles; and some, prophets; and some, evangelists; and some, pastors and teachers." Ephesians 4:8–11.

18. *What general rule is laid down for testing all prophets?*
"To the law and to the testimony: If they speak not according to this word, it is because there is no light in them." Isaiah 8:20.

19. *What gift will characterize the last, or remnant, church?*
"And the dragon was wroth with the woman, and went to make war with the remnant of her seed, which keep the commandments of God, and have the testimony of Jesus Christ." Revelation 12:17. "The testimony of Jesus is the spirit of prophecy." Revelation 19:10. (See also Revelation 22:9.)

Note: The term "spirit of prophecy" occurs only once in the Holy Scriptures. But it is found in ancient Jewish

writings. The meaning is "gift of prophecy." Two examples
are cited here.

"The Targum of Jonathan on 2 Samuel 23:2 reads:

" 'David said, By the Spirit of Prophecy of Jehovah I speak
these things.'—Quoted in Appendix Note IV to 2 Samuel in
The Cambridge Bible for Schools and Colleges (Cambridge:
University Press, 1899), page 237.

"The *Pulpit Commentary* remarks:

" 'David, in his last days, like Jacob and Moses, received
the spirit of prophecy.' On 2 Samuel 23:1–7."

According to Bible teaching, the gift of prophecy or "the
spirit of prophecy" was to reappear in modern times. See
Joel 2:28–30.

20. *What is the promised result of believing God's prophet?*
"Believe in the Lord your God, so shall ye be established;
believe His prophets, so shall ye prosper." 2 Chronicles 20:20.

Whatever, Jeane Dixon's record of accuracy is unequaled.

Witness the following predictions which have come to pass
as previously reported in Ruth Montgomery's book about
Jeane Dixon, *A Gift of Prophecy*.

In the fall of 1944 Jeane Dixon predicted that "China will
go Communist and become our greatest trouble. Africa will
be our next biggest worry in the foreign field." She told this
to President Roosevelt during a private meeting at the White
House. At that time Roosevelt disagreed. The political developments in the years immediately following proved her
right.

Another startling prediction took place in 1945 while she
was talking to a high-ranking official of the Indian diplomatic
mission in Washington.

"On June second, 1947, your country, India, will split in
two as the result of an internal controversy."

Utter bewilderment!

"Impossible," the official shouted. "My country will never
be divided!"

But on June 2, 1947, the headlines of the world's newspapers announced the division of this former part of the British Empire.

Her next prophecy was more shocking. It too dealt with India and took place during the summer of 1947 when, listening to a conversation between her husband and a friend, she suddenly exclaimed, "Mahatma Gandhi will be assassinated within the next six months. He will be killed by someone they least suspect."

The record speaks for itself. A Hindu fanatic *did* assassinate India's spiritual leader, a short six months later. The assassin? A man who up until that time had been beyond suspicion!

Other predictions followed in quick succession. Marilyn Monroe's suicide was announced by Jeane in late 1961, and when I mourned the death of a friend, Bill Ronallo, private bodyguard to the UN's Secretary General Dag Hammarskjöld, in mid-September of that year, it was because I hadn't known of Jeane's prediction months before when she warned a friend, Eleanor Bumgardner, "Whatever you do this summer—don't fly in the same plane with Dag Hammarskjöld in mid-September, for this plane will crash and he will be killed."

While Jeane Dixon's international predictions made the headlines of papers around the world, her national predictions received as much publicity right here in the United States.

She predicted among other things the merger of the AFL and the CIO, the defeat of Dewey by Harry Truman, the landslide election of Dwight D. Eisenhower, the fall of Nikita Khrushchev, the "birth" of the first Sputnik, the death of Secretary of State John Foster Dulles, and many other cataclysmic events which have shaped our times.

In the eyes of the public, however, these were surpassed by the dramatic prediction of the death of John F. Kennedy.

It was the end of a story that started eleven years before the fatal bullet struck down and killed JFK.

"It was one of those drizzly rainy mornings," Jeane told us, "when I entered St. Matthew's Cathedral in Washington, D.C., for my morning devotion. I felt a glow of anticipation —a feeling that had been with me for several days. It was a feeling of expectancy, as if something momentous was going to happen and I would be involved. . . .

"I remember standing in front of the statue of the Virgin Mary when suddenly the White House appeared before me in dazzling brightness. Coming out of a haze, the numerals 1-9-6-0 formed above the roof. An ominous dark cloud appeared, covering the numbers, and dripped slowly onto the White House . . . Then I looked down and saw a young man, tall and blue-eyed, crowned with a shock of thick brown hair, quietly standing in front of the main door.

"I was still staring at him when a voice came out of nowhere, telling me softly that this young man, a Democrat, to be seated as President in 1960, would be assassinated while in office.

"The vision faded into the wall—into the distance as softly as it had come," Jeane recalled, "but it stayed with me until that fatal day in Dallas when it was fulfilled."

A more recent event, the Republican victory at the polls, was predicted by her as early as 1963.

"The Republican party will make great strides in the South," she said at that time. "It will put forth tremendous efforts to come closer to the people and will defeat the Democratic party in six years."

There is a man in the White House today who will vouch for Jeane Dixon's accuracy a full 100 percent!

The visions experienced by Jeane Dixon since the publication of *A Gift of Prophecy*, in 1965, are even more startling, more threatening, and more premonitory than ever before. They not only cover recent events already come true; they

take us all the way to the year 1999, when, she says, a cross
will appear in the eastern skies, and beyond 1999 when humanity will be called to judgment.

Let us observe history in the making before the historians
get a glimpse of it, for such is the power of prophecy.

Bloomfield, Mich.

RENE NOORBERGEN

1

Facets of a Busy Life

For over two decades now my husband Jimmy and I have
lived in our Victorian-style house in the northwest section of
Washington, D.C., and I have loved every moment of it.

Our home is one of those unpretentious white, brick-row
houses that was so fashionable in the 1870's, when it was
built. Nearly a hundred years have gone by since then, and
it has acquired an intangible loveliness that can be felt instead of seen. The house has gradually become a part of all
the lives of those who lived within its walls, and seems to
embrace me with a glowing tenderness whenever I enter.

We had been searching for a place like this for quite some
time; however, when we found it, Jimmy did not immediately share my enthusiasm, but soon became as charmed with
it as I.

The moment one leaves the sidewalk and enters our little
front garden through a delicate wrought-iron gate, the decades vanish, and the pebble path that encircles the tiny flower
beds helps to bring the Victorian era of its origin much closer.

Let me share this simple joy with you on a "brief guided
tour."

We start with the reception room immediately to the right
of the foyer, where in the wintertime a log fire adds warmth
to the already cozy atmosphere, highlighted by an antique
Dutch sleigh filled with flowering plants.

Behind it, past the staircase, is our French dining room, with doors that open onto the rear garden. This room is enhanced by an antique crystal chandelier centered over the table. A gleaming silver basket, always filled with fresh flowers (often sent to us), reflects the sparkling light of the chandelier in a thousand rays.

The entire first floor is covered with white marble—for practical purposes. While in the process of renovating the house, the workmen found hordes of termites occupying our wooden floors, and reflooring with marble was the only way to outwit them. The marble adds to the Mediterranean feeling that permeates the lower section of the house.

Our small gold and white drawing room on the second floor overlooks the front garden and is furnished mostly with French pieces which Jimmy and I have inherited. In addition there are some pieces we have collected.

To the right of the upstairs foyer is our combination library-music room, decorated in black, gold, and a cool, pale green. Jimmy's piano and desk are here, also several thousand books which line the shelves of the fireplace wall. Chairs and a sofa are placed around the large coffee table standing before the fireplace, flanked by cupboards with black double doors garnished by ornately designed brass handles.

I do not know the actual count of the books we own . . . I only know there is not one book on psychic phenomena among them.

Not too long ago Jackie Gleason surprised me one evening with a phone call and during our conversation mentioned that he owned over a thousand books on psychic phenomena. When I told him that I did not own *one,* he sounded shocked.

"You're for real, I guess . . ." he replied. "You *must* be."

On the third floor of our house are our bedrooms. In the front one overlooking the garden is my lace-canopied bed which once belonged to Empress Eugénie of France. On the pale-blue wall hangs a handmade gold crucifix, sent to me years ago by the late German Chancellor Conrad Adenauer.

The décor of the other master bedroom is rose, gold, and black. The canopied bed in which Calvin Coolidge once slept came from the estate of the late Cissy Patterson, a member of the famous Chicago newspaper family. It was a gift to me from Ruth Montgomery who purchased it from the Patterson estate.

The fourth floor of our home contains our guest room and the rooms of our chatelaine, Miss Susan. The top floor is used for storage.

It is a comfortable house, and I love puttering about in it. Yet it seems most of my life is consumed working in our real estate office.

My working days are long and are spent concentrating on my responsibilities as Secretary-Treasurer of James L. Dixon & Company, supervising the ever-broadening activities of Children to Children, Inc., and working closely with my staff on the personal correspondence from thousands of people who want to know "what will happen."

In a normal forty-hour work week there would be no time to answer any of these letters. In fact, if I were limited by union regulations as to how many hours I could work each week, much of what I now do would be only a hope—not a reality—in my life.

So many people have asked me, "How do you find the time?" I have computed my working year in an effort to answer them.

I work fifty-two Saturdays and fifty-two Sundays (these are peak days of our service to people searching for homes), and I work on nine holidays of the year (never Christmas). That totals 113 days on which most people do not work at their "business of living." Added to that is a two-week vacation period, or fourteen days (which I never take), making a total of 127 days. To this I add another ninety days—representing the total annual minimum overtime (I never work less than ten hours a day)—arriving at the grand total of 217 extra days of working time in every year. That is how I find the time.

The evenings I am not at the office are spent fulfilling speaking engagements, making television appearances or cutting tapes for future shows, attending business dinners, casting my horoscope columns, visiting with the children cared for by our Foundation, and granting special interviews for magazine and newspaper articles. Whenever, for reasons of expediency, these activities are inserted into my working day, the time must be made up at my desk.

One such incident—which demanded immediate time away from my normal working day because of the circumstances and individuals involved—was a request from the Houston *Post* to meditate on the astronauts who orbited the moon in May of 1969. "Please meditate," they asked, "and tell us all you can quickly about these three astronauts."

Leaving work early that night, I shut myself in my room to pray and meditate.

My psychic findings on the astronauts were published a day later, May 21, 1969, among them my forecast that Commander Stafford would somehow find his skin would "become a little irritated."

Two days later newspapers around the world carried excerpts of the astronauts' reports over the space-to-earth communicator, including a complaint by Commander Stafford that his face was "itching and irritated."

Later, investigation revealed that tiny particles of fiberglass had separated from the cabin of the spaceship and embedded themselves in his face.

Public appearances take much of my time, but I welcome every one of them, for the contributions received from these appearances are always turned over entirely to Children to Children.

I do not recommend that everybody should have such long

working hours. But I strive to be in harmony with whatever I am doing at the moment, so that I would rather be doing that particular thing more than anything else at that particular moment!

When the flood of letters from people seeking my help became so huge that it was absolutely impossible to answer every letter personally—much as I wanted to—the thought came to me, "If only there were some way I could offer people a general guideline for their daily lives . . . if I could somehow chart an overall course of living . . . many of these people could use it to help and guide themselves, and would not then need a personal reply from me."

So "Jeane Dixon's Horoscope Column" was born.

I sincerely believe that my daily general horoscope columns reflect a guideline for some people which, if followed reasonably, can beneficially affect their daily lives.

The science of astrology was taught me as a child by Father Henry, a consecrated, dedicated Jesuit priest at Loyola University in California, and it was through his teachings as well as his exemplary goodness that I came to believe it is possible also to help people through such astrological knowledge.

My home life is a happy one. Our friends often speak of the peace and tranquillity that seem to permeate our home. This feeling, in the house when we bought it, has prevailed, I hope, due to the harmonious way in which my husband Jimmy and I have tried to pursue our life together and yet preserve our individual identities. Miss Susan came to me one day after she had been with us for several months and asked, puzzled:

"Mrs. Dixon, don't you and Mr. Dixon ever quarrel or argue?"

Our relationship surprised her, yet to us it is natural. Like all married couples, we do have our disagreements, but we have found an effective way to keep them from becoming a major issue. We both realize that the best way to dispel an argumentative mood is not to give in to it, so with a polite excuse one of us leaves the room (it seems always to be me), and the potential argument dies.

Thoughtful as my husband is, he has still another way to convey his point to me about matters he considers most delicate. He leaves a note for me, giving me the advantage of thinking over his opinion before we meet again later on, by which time I will have been able to give his position careful consideration.

However, should whatever Jimmy proposes be something to which I get a negative psychic reaction, I let him know immediately, for a psychic reaction to me is more important than any personal consideration.

He accepts my "foresight" very matter-of-factly.

"God gives different talents to different people. One of Jeane's talents is her psychic gift," he has been heard to remark on occasion. "God gives different talents to different people, just as He also gives different crosses to bear."

It is not the talents and the crosses we are given—it is what we *do* with our talents and crosses that counts!

Although Jimmy is a businessman, he is nevertheless vehemently opposed to my accepting financial rewards for my "readings" or accepting one of the many commercial television ventures constantly offered me. Monetary gifts that do come in from people who appreciate any help I may have given them through the use of my psychic ability go into the general fund of Children to Children, Inc.

Living two productive lives is very demanding. Jimmy, realizing the strain it could place on me, often suggests that I retire from the real estate business and devote myself entirely to the foundation and my psychic work.

This to me is impossible. I would feel out of touch with life if I were to be removed from the realities of the business world. There is also another factor which I deem even more important. God gave me a talent for business also, and I cannot refute His will by refusing to develop and utilize that talent.

Jimmy realizes this, yet he worries because he cares.

To those who do not know him well, he appears every inch a businessman. He is conservative, accustomed to making decisions under pressure, and presents a cool, businesslike façade to the outside world. Those who know him, however, are aware that a soft, tender heart beats underneath this stern countenance and that he is as sympathetic as he is realistic.

He is not a man of many words, yet his tenderness is touching. Every evening, for example, I find a deep-red rose lying on my pillow, placed there by Jimmy as a token of his love. If red roses are not available, then he may switch to a soft pink one, but it is always a rose. He started this early in our marriage and has never forgotten.

He was asked why he keeps this up so unceasingly. His answer was simple and direct.

"Because I love her."

When I must be out of town and do not plan to return that night, Jimmy always gives me a card with a picture of a rose on it, with the words, "Bon Voyage," and signs it, "I love you . . ."

He has a way of twisting me around the tip of his little finger.

Twenty-three years ago, when I returned from a long trip, he greeted me at the airport and tenderly said, "I missed you," while at the same time slipping a small flat box into my hand.

In it was one of the most beautiful gifts he has ever given me.

It was a slim cross made of yellow gold and enhanced with exquisite Russian amethysts. In physical size it was only two inches long, but the beauty and feel of it vibrated all the way to heaven. Jimmy had purchased it from Emerich Korecz, a scholarly rare-antique expert who told him it had once been part of the estate of Mrs. Robert E. Lee. Prior to that it had belonged to a bishop of the Russian Orthodox Church.

The cross has become an integral part of my life. I wear it on a delicate golden chain, and it serves as a constant reminder to me that in all affairs of life we are dependent on the grace of the cross.

I would enjoy surprising Jimmy with presents, but this is not the easiest thing to do as he feels he has everything he needs.

This does not prevent him, though, from surprising me with gifts. In fact, some of my favorite articles of clothing have been given me by Jimmy who brought them home because, as he puts it, "I just couldn't imagine you without them."

My taste in clothes is simple. Most of my suits or coats have pockets for the specific purpose of carrying the cards with names of those who have requested me to include them in my prayers. I am conscious of clothes, yet I am not a slave to them. Time and time again I leave a new dress hanging in my closet while I choose an old favorite to wear.

One of the blessings of our marriage, I feel, is our mutual love for animals. Jimmy could no more turn away a stray cat or dog than I could, and although he can be extremely practical about household expenses, I have never known him to pose any objections to our sometimes excessively high veterinary bills.

Not so long ago, I recall that for a period of about ten days, Jimmy used to leave the house every morning with a hamburger patty wrapped in paper and a small container of milk to feed a half-starved stray cat he found hiding under a hedge near an abandoned house.

And then there is Mike, our cat. He has so brightened our lives that we call him Mike the MagiCat.

Mike's mother was thought to be a tomcat by the family who adopted her. They did not find that "he" was a "she" until she had given birth to three kittens on the French sofa in their drawing room!

They took one look at the young intruders and decided that something would have to be done.

"Let's get rid of the ugly one," the maid suggested, "and keep the blue and the black one."

When I heard of this, I asked for the ugly one. I got it, and he has proved to be a constant source of surprises ever since.

He was a problem right from the start, for like all young bloods he was a rover—but one with class! At least he knew where he was heading.

He showed this the first time he ran away. He did not come back by himself—oh no! He wanted a reward to be offered for him, and so it was. A display ad using his photograph and offering a reward for his return in the Washington papers quickly brought results. Guards at the northwest gate of the White House soon notified me that they had found Mike, wandering about the White House grounds. Ignoring their orders (which read that stray animals would have to be turned over to the Animal Rescue League at once), they took Mike into "protective custody" until I claimed him.

He must have liked the bits of meat and fish they fed him while holding him in custody, for two days later he ran away again. This time he was returned in a White House limousine accompanied by two bodyguards!

Mike has to share our affection with many other animals we have taken under our wings.

Peggy is one of them.

It was about four o'clock on a chilly, rainy afternoon when a woman, who lives not far from us and who must have heard about our love for animals, called me at my office.

"A little black puppy is lying in the gutter close to your house," she reported to me. "I think it has been run over, for it does nothing but cry and whimper."

Victor Rand, Jimmy's secretary, rushed over and brought the whimpering pup to me.

She was trembling fearfully, and it seemed that one of her legs was broken. An examination by Dr. William Larson of the Friendship Animal Hospital revealed that she had three broken ribs also.

I can still remember that sad, mournful look in her eyes when we left her in the care of Dr. Larson. She remained at the hospital until her ribs had knit. Her leg was still in a splint, but that did not prevent us from taking her home and showering her with affection and care.

Have you ever seen a little puppy try to express her dog-felt thanks by attempting to shake hands with a splinted leg?

Peggy tried it, and with that one little handshake she won for herself a lasting place in our hearts.

When Jimmy and I first came to Washington in 1942 I used to "read" for servicemen at the Home Hospitality Parties hosted by Mrs. Martin Vogel. As time went by and more and more people heard about my psychic gift, I became deluged with requests for help from people unknown to me. Among the many who sought my advice were members of top circles of government, statesmen, ambassadors, and visiting dignitaries. My reputation for reliability spread, and when my predictions were eventually published in newspapers across the nation, telephone calls, telegrams, and letters flooded my office and home unceasingly. It was the widespread publicity following my prophecy of the death of President John F. Kennedy, however, that made me well known, both here and abroad.

The publication of *A Gift of Prophecy*—the book about me by Ruth Montgomery—also caused much comment and publicity, resulting in even more mail!

Expressions of fear, worries concerning loved ones, requests for tips on the stock market, all started pouring into my office. The letters now average approximately three thousand a week, but there have been times when a thousand letters a day followed some unusual prediction or event. My daily horoscope column, appearing in over three hundred newspapers in the United States, and my frequent lectures have also added hundreds of letters to our daily delivery.

Some of the letters are interesting; others are pathetic.

"Dear Mrs. Dixon," one began, "I hear how you read for a lot of important people so I guess you wouldn't be interested in reading for an average man who earns his living as a writer. In 'The Gift of Prophecy' Ruth Montgomery tells how you deal with the big shots; diplomats, movie stars, TV stars, and the like. Well, if the sale of your book depended only on the important names you think so highly of, it wouldn't make much money for you, that's for sure. A woman with your gift casts a spell of hope for poor people. But you don't give them this help. Only for celebrities and the rich do you leave your real estate office. I guess I'd better wait until I get rich and famous before asking your help."

The sender of this letter was no doubt sincere in his feelings, but he was wrong. This was one of the many letters to which I could not refuse a reply.

"Thank you for your letter," I wrote. "It is only because I read for some people who are prominent that you have ever heard of me. I also read for many who are not prominent and who, indeed, have no desire to be. During World War II, I read for the soldiers who were going off to defend our country and for those who had come home broken in body, mind and spirit. The noncommissioned officers were my 'big shots.' However, when I am summoned to the White House or to Capitol Hill, it is reported as news and then you do hear about my reading for some V.I.P.

"Above all, I do my best to help people help themselves. Each one of us has to discover his talent and develop it. You have expressed yourself graphically . . . and this would indicate to me that you are in the right field . . . have found your talent and are using it.

"How nice it would be if I had the time that it takes to

meditate for you; but because of the many, many demands upon my time and person it has become impossible to do so.

"In the future I hope to be able to apportion my days so that I can set aside one day a week to talk with people and try to help them with their problems.

"I ask for your prayers and shall remember you in mine. Please do not lose your faith."

Another correspondent with such deep-seated trust in my psychic gift that she felt it unnecessary to explain her problem wrote:

"Dear Jeane Dixon,

"Your book proves your God-given talent is wonderful. I know you are busy for I read all about that. But I beg you to take a little time and come up with an answer to my problem.

"I assure you the situation I'm involved in and the unjust decision is making me ill.

"My birthday is May 3, 1930.

"Please help me."

Another letter was filled with even more trust—although the skeptical writer did not dare admit it.

"Dear Mrs. Dixon," he began. "I enjoyed your book on prophecy, but I admit I am skeptical about some of the things you are supposed to have seen. If you can really predict things before they happen, will you please tell me the past, present and future and especially about a business deal I want to put over. Thanks!"

I am asked recurringly if I believe in psychic phenomena. Yes, I do. I often compare my instinct for things unseen to the instinct of an artist for color balance and beauty.

The feeling of extrasensory phenomena is a part of life and can no more be disregarded than light or darkness, because there are so many V.I.U.'s—Very Important Unknowns.

Many of us upon entering a house—whether it be vacant or occupied—have gone through the experience of feeling, "I just love this place!" while other places give us the feeling, "I do not like this place!" And when asked why, we can seldom give a satisfactory answer. Oftentimes we undergo these feelings before we have even entered a house; it is a something based on other than practical considerations. It is more of a conscious response to an unconscious reaction we have because of certain vibrations that the house emanates.

There is a respected theory that wood, because of its cellular make-up, is capable of absorbing sounds and other vibrations. Since wood reacts to atmospheric conditions and expands in hot, moist weather and contracts in cold, dry weather, this theory would explain in part why many people think apparitions appear only in certain seasons, for it is then that they are conscious of the apparitions.

Every nation has its favorite ghost stories. As individuals, many of *us* have our own favorite story or, for that matter, our own "private" ghost.

Our family's "ghost" was my mother's beloved black-and-white collie named "Shep." Shep was a magnificent dog, but his life was all too short. He was poisoned by a neighbor who did not like animals.

I remember vividly a stormy night several weeks after Shep died. We were all sitting before a crackling log fire when we heard a scratching and whining at the door.

Mother jumped up.

"There's Shep," she cried out. "I hear Shep!"

She threw open the door, but all she found was the howling wind and banks of snow—Shep was not there.

We heard him many evenings after that stormy night, always scratching, always whining. I believe that we loved him so much we continually tried to bring him back. Of course, he could not come back, he was gone forever.

One of my favorite ghost stories was told to me by a young man whose word I would not doubt. He had been overseas with the Army and returned to New England to discover that his parents had moved into a house dating back to 1678. They had purchased it while he was away but never said much about it.

His real introduction came when he was alone one evening in the old mansion. He picked up a book and went to bed to read.

Within minutes his reading was interrupted by the sounds of soft, shuffling footsteps in the hall, followed by a woman's persistent weeping.

Had his mother come back? Had something happened to her? He jumped out of bed and ran toward the door.

The crying was louder now . . .

He opened the door and stared into an empty hallway. The footsteps had ceased, but the crying was still there, only it had changed to a soft whimpering. It emanated from a bricked-up fireplace right across from his bedroom door.

When his parents returned they found him sitting downstairs watching television with all the lights in the house ablaze.

"We purposely did not tell you about our 'ghost,'" his mother explained after he had told them about the crying woman. "We have heard her many times but wanted you to find out about her for yourself."

Who she is supposed to be, no one knows.

I recall a letter that came in some time around the middle of last year, in which the writer requested information about a missing son. Mental anguish always concerns me, so I meditated at once, hoping to pick up the missing boy's vibrations. Vibrations mean there is life; absence of vibrations means life is gone.

Sometimes the awareness of life or death comes to me before I have even completely read the letter; sometimes merely touching it is sufficient contact to bring me in touch with the missing person's vibrations. Sometimes I do not get any immediate vibrations, and not having the time that it takes to meditate, I cannot give any psychic information on the missing person.

The above letter, however, "told" me at once that the young man who had already been missing for over five weeks was alive, but all further information eluded me.

I placed the letter in my active file and promised myself to give it more attention later on in the day. Further concentration during a quiet part of the day often brings more definite results.

Nothing happened that day even though my mind was filled with the suffering of the frantic parents.

The answer came the next day. While working at my desk, I suddenly called to Victor Rand:

"Mr. Rand . . . I have something!"

"What is it?" he asked quickly. "What is it about?"

"The young boy who is missing . . . the young boy about whom I had a letter yesterday. I just saw him. He is alive. I see him surrounded by flowers and shrubbery . . . He is not far from his house, either. I can see him as plain as day . . ."

"Any more details?"

"Not for now. I may know more before the end of the day, but let's not wait for that. We must send his mother a letter immediately, telling her what I have seen . . . telling her I see him living in a garden . . ."

I breathed a sigh of relief when the letter left my office, for I could well understand her anxiety.

A few days later I received confirmation of what I had "seen."

His mother notified me that she had found her son. Deciding to make his parents unhappy for reasons known only to him, the young man had moved a few of his elementary belongings into an empty room above a garage located at the foot of the garden. Strangely enough, his mother had no inkling of this, even though he stayed alive by nightly raids on the family refrigerator.

She discovered him when, driven by an unknown impulse

(her own ESP at work?), she decided to take a look at the empty garage. Hearing noises upstairs, she investigated the spare room and found her son. . . .

Some of the most difficult letters to answer are those about missing persons of whom I pick up no vibrations.

I recall a woman whose husband had disappeared while flying to a destination outside of the United States. She wrote that she had not heard a word from him since he had taken off in his airplane. Hoping that I might be able to locate him, she sent me his intended routing, a complete description of him and his plane, and some of his personal belongings.

I concentrated long and carefully but could not detect his vibrations—I received no sign of life.

With a sad and heavy heart I finally sat down behind my typewriter.

"I wish with all my heart I had some news of your husband for you," I wrote, "but I am unable to pick up any of his vibrations. All of the things you sent me are being returned for I know you will want to keep them. I shall say special prayers for you and your children."

A short time later the charred remains of the plane and her husband's body were found in a desolate mountain pass where he had crashed.

There is an infinite variety to what my correspondents ask. Yet the fact that they are *moved* to write—together with the emotions they reveal in the *way* they write—bespeaks how important their problems are to them.

A mother wrote asking if I could locate the pictures of her son's first Communion. "I photographed him as he approached the altar," she wrote proudly, "in that beautifully reverent moment when he received God's blessing, and when he walked along the rail back to me. The film," she continued, "has been lost or mislaid in the developing lab. Is it lost for good? Can it have been destroyed? Or can it possibly be somewhere in a mail chute?"

Her worries became mine, yet this one, like others, did not have an immediate answer waiting for it.

Occasionally I am asked to meditate on a complete list of items, and although I would like to oblige, it is virtually impossible to fulfill every request.

"Would you," one letter asked, "make predictions for me, giving special attention about my chances for (a) future finances, (b) foreign travel, (c) marriage, and (d) education?"

About one-third of all my letter writers ask for guidance in finding their talents and their individual purposes in life. Many of these people are truly concerned about their place in life, and I try to help them whenever I can. The largest number of letters are those with which we are deluged whenever a false rumor is rampant. When this happens, our mail increases dramatically and the Dixon Company's switchboard is so jammed it becomes practically impossible for us to conduct our real estate business.

More important, however, is the unnecessary fear and worry these rumors cause in the hearts of many thousands.

Our mail has never been heavier or our switchboard more jammed than in 1964 when someone spread the rumor that I had predicted the crash of a plane in which the Beatles would travel. I had not.

In the winter of 1967 someone claimed that I had foreseen a horde of Martians descending upon earth to carry off our children and teen-age girls. Although this seemed too far fetched to be ranked even as science fiction, many were truly alarmed.

Another rumor hit hard in the spring of 1967. Those who had sons or husbands or sweethearts in the Coast Guard's "Operation Charlie" spent many sleepless nights and fearful days because of a persistent rumor that I had predicted that the ship of this operation would go down off Newfoundland and all aboard would be lost. Operation Charlie, however, terminated successfully and the ship returned safely.

Not long after the opening of Expo '67 I was besieged with

letters, telegrams, and telephone calls inquiring whether it was true that I had foretold that the man-made island holding the exposition would sink with a loss of life that rose—as the rumor snowballed—from 1500 to 8000 people!

The inquiries came largely from people throughout the United States and Canada, for many of them planned a trip to Expo '67. Others had relatives residing in the Expo area. Also many letters came from hotels and motels in the area that were dependent on the tourist trade.

The pressure became so immense that I finally asked the editor of the Montreal *Gazette* to deny this rumor for me.

Another false rumor that made headlines was the one about the destruction of Guam. A soldier stationed in San Francisco at the time of the rumor was extremely concerned about this "prediction" and phoned me for either a denial or a confirmation. I informed him that I had said nothing of the kind. Another member of the armed forces wrote me from Okinawa asking whether there was any truth in my prediction that Okinawa would gradually disappear beneath the waves.

The most fantastic rumors are no doubt created by some very imaginative people, and it is puzzling why they accredit these wild tales to me. Two years ago a fifteen-year-old girl sent me a frantic letter, inquiring whether it was true that I had predicted that all girls with pierced ears would die in June 1979 of a strange, fatal disease. Of course it wasn't true. I answered her immediately and told her there was not one word of truth in it! But I answered hundreds of letters about this before it died down.

More recently, in March and April of 1969, another wild rumor was set in motion. Devastating earthquakes had been predicted for Southern California, and as is often the case, many people credited me with having made this ominous prediction.

On April 1 I called a press conference to issue the following denial:

"During the past several weeks, my syndicate, Newsday

Specials, and I have received more than 50 telephone calls a day and hundreds of letters and telegrams from all over the country, asking about the validity of the widespread rumors —erroneously attributed to me—that I had predicted that in the near future, California—or a large portion of that state— will slide into the Pacific Ocean.

"Numerous radio and television personalities—as well as many segments of the press—have circulated the belief that I had indeed predicted such a catastrophe.

"At this time I should like to make it perfectly clear to the news media, and through that media to my fellow Americans, that at NO time have I ever predicted—nor do I predict—that such a cataclysm is imminent.

"I do not say that there will not be earthquakes or tremors, but I repeat I have not predicted—and do not now predict— such a grave occurrence as the imminent disappearance of California."

I doubt that false rumors are ever conceived or spread maliciously. More than likely, I think they are disseminated by young people who crave attention and a sense of importance, and who—because they are bored—think it would be fun to stir up a little mischief.

Generally it is impossible to trace rumors to their sources. We did, however, after much work, succeed in locating the origin of that Martian tale. It began when a teen-age baby-sitter in Baltimore, a devout follower of science-fiction programs, threatened her two charges with the invasion of the Martians if they would not go to bed.

"Who said the Martians would come and get us?" they squealed defiantly when she confronted them with the threat.

"Jeane Dixon," she answered bluntly.

Within minutes the two were in bed—but that was not the end of the story.

The next morning they told their parents that the Martians were coming and that I had said so. They spread the same story at school, and before they were tucked in bed that night, the rumor had gotten out of hand, and hundreds of frightened children crawled under their blankets—wondering when the Martians would come. . . .

No harm was meant, but harm was done in the hearts of little innocent ones because of a desperate baby-sitter.

Children have always been dear to my heart, and I often think back to that unseasonably raw autumn day some twenty-odd Octobers ago when, shivering inside my otherwise warm tweed coat, I drove through the Virginia countryside searching for a house—any house—with a telephone line leading to it.

I had been out in the country most of the day, house-hunting for a country place. Since my husband had gone on a business trip, this seemed to be the ideal time for it.

A flat tire spoiled my plans and I needed a telephone to call for road service. I had just about given up all hope of ever finding a telephone when I spied a telephone line leading to a small white house.

After my call was completed, and I was preparing to leave, several little Negro children came charging out of a small henhouse in the back yard. I learned in talking with them that they lived there with their mother and grandmother . . .

The children were in need of help in many ways.

When my husband returned from his business trip, I discussed their sad plight with him, and armed with his blessing and financial aid, I made a detailed list of what I felt was needed. There had to be a stove, a new and adequate diet, warm clothing, etc. I also had to supply soap, brushes, a sewing kit, shoe polish—in short, some of the things that are so necessary. Teaching them mental and physical hygiene was another opportunity to help them—another privilege for me.

On one of my semi-weekly visits I was asked by the mother if I could arrange for her to receive a larger relief check.

"A woman down the road who has a smaller family than

I do gets a lot more than me," she said. "How can I get a bigger one?"

"Do you think the government owes you money you didn't earn?" I answered, trying to make her think.

"Yes," she replied vehemently. "They promised me bigger relief checks if I voted for —— and he won!"

With hopeful faces the children had listened to our conversation, yet when it became obvious that I would not supply the additional money that could mean all the things they never had, their faces dropped.

I turned to the older boy—he seemed about sixteen or seventeen—and asked, "Do you realize the good Lord has given you a talent that will be yours as long as you live, and that this talent will earn money for you if you will learn how to use it?"

"But Abraham Lincoln said we were all created equal," the boy replied.

I looked at him and smiled. "Yes, he did say that . . . and he was quoting Thomas Jefferson. But our Lord did not say that we were all created equal. We are all His children, but we are not equal in intelligence, we are not equal in talent, and we are not equal in circumstances. We are, however, equal in the sight of our Creator because He loves each one of us. We are equal in the fact that He has given to each one of us particular gifts—particular talents—in order to accomplish a particular purpose. We are equal insofar as God will always help each one of us to accomplish our purpose by developing and using our talents. In that sense we are equal. But since there has never been anyone exactly like you with your particular talent and your particular purpose, no one is equal to you. You are *special*."

A tiny glimmer of hope came into his eyes as the true meaning of what I had said became clear to him.

"Can you help me find my talent?" he asked timidly. And so we sat down and talked.

There in the henhouse we discussed his future and the

future of the members of his family. The little round stove I had purchased for them tried its best to heat the cramped ten-by-twelve-foot area, but the cold draft that seemed to come from everywhere made it grossly inadequate. The room was scantily furnished. Two cots in the corner of the room and the bench I sat on were just about all they possessed, but we managed. We talked—and their spirits brightened as I told them of the outside world and God's Divine Plan for each one of us.

With the assistance that I—and others—supplied, they soon began to experience a change in their lives. By January the two older children were sufficiently ready to go to school, and since there was no Negro school within walking distance of the henhouse, I arranged for the white children who lived nearby to take them along to their school.

"When the teacher asks you what you want," I instructed them, "say, ever so politely, 'We just want to learn, please, thank you, ma'am.'"

It was my own way of introducing integration and it worked.

Arrangements were also made for the children to go to Sunday School. One of the little ones, knowing that I was a Roman Catholic, wanted to become one too. There was no Catholic church in the vicinity, but I told her that what counted was not which church she attended, but rather her thoughts, words, and deeds during every single day of her life. I told her to begin each day with thanks to God for being alive, then to pray as if everything depended on God and work as if everything depended on her.

Another important change was made. An older boy who lived away from home was asked to come back. No one had figured out as yet where he would be sleeping, but I felt it essential for him to be there as we made the changes, so that he might move forward with the others and not remain behind socially and spiritually.

Through the years I have kept in close touch with this

family. When the oldest girl was ready to graduate from high school another milestone was reached. Her prom marked the first time the mother or the grandmother had ever been inside a school, and every time the girl danced past them, their eyes brightened with pride and their beaming faces reflected an inner happiness.

The beginning of Children to Children, Inc., formally organized many autumns later in 1964, was influenced by my rewarding experiences with this family.

Once they had understood that they could learn to *learn*, and then learn to *earn*, they made rapid progress. It was not long before they ceased to look to national, state, or local governments for help and were proud to stand firmly on their own accomplishments.

Today all the children of this family have already demonstrated a strong instinct to help others less fortunate.

The children of today will be the citizens of tomorrow and must be given every chance and every opportunity to develop to their full potential if the world is to know peace and harmony.

With this concept as a basis, the aims of Children to Children, Inc., have been formulated as follows,

* HELP CHILDREN discover the wonder of God and grow spiritually in the religion of their choice, giving them *faith*.
* HELP CHILDREN by endeavoring to cure many of the ills and diseases that afflict them, so their minds and bodies may grow strong and healthy.
* HELP CHILDREN help themselves to find their talents and develop them as they develop their minds and bodies so that, as they mature, they may lead fruitful lives and contribute to the lives of others.
* HELP CHILDREN know the true meaning of the word *love*, as God has commanded.

Through love and understanding we learn to live in harmony with God's plan for this universe of man.

Currently much of my attention and practically all of my resources are being directed toward the realization of one of my most memorable psychic visions: erection of the Jeane Dixon Medical Center. This center, as I have "seen" it and as it now exists in an architect's model, will be built in the shape of a wagon wheel.

It will contain the most advanced and sophisticated laboratory facilities available to man, including computerized research systems.

Each of the eight spokes of the "wheel" will be reserved for the treatment of specific children's diseases. Leukemia, cancer, heart and nervous disorders are among those that will be housed in the special wings. Between the spokes—which will be several stories high with each successive level recessed so as to provide individual "floor terraces"—will be carefully and expertly landscaped lawns or children's zoos, created solely and especially for the enjoyment of the little ones.

The lower floor of the eight spokes will meet at the all-faiths chapel to be constructed in the hub of the wheel. The exterior will be covered with stained glass, crowned with a soaring spire tipped by an eternal flame. . . .

It is a gigantic project, but with the help of God, all is possible.

At times I have said that had I known at the beginning there would be a million steps instead of five hundred involved in getting Children to Children, Inc., established, I might have left it to the government and its vast resources. But this is not really so. I am fully convinced that Divine Guidance moved me in this direction.

When, after my "first" family was helped, the cost of aiding the needy rose beyond what my husband and I could supply, I decided to channel the earnings of my psychic gift into this project. Previously this money had been donated to the Damon Runyon Fund and other charities. However, since the inception of Children to Children, Inc., the Foundation has received the remuneration I earn from speaking engagements, radio or television appearances, etc.

Whenever I think back to that chilly autumn day when the family in the abandoned henhouse became the cornerstone, so to speak, of Children to Children, Inc., I am impressed at how inconspicuous the start of anything can be.

Some things, however, begin auspiciously—with a sign—like the coming of a dove through terrace doors.

2

The Dove

It was my old friend, Victor Werner, who unknowingly set the stage for one of my most surprising visions.

Mr. Werner came to see me one day and during our conversation proudly told me that he was about to receive a medal which had been awarded to him at the close of World War I by King Albert of Belgium. Naturally I wondered out loud why he had never before received it.

As the story developed, I became aware that Mr. Werner, who was retiring from the Civil Service, had been very influential in solidifying the friendly relations between Belgium and the United States in the postwar period, and as an expression of his appreciation, King Albert had honored him with the silver medal in the Order of King Leopold II.

However, even though this award had been officially granted, Mr. Werner never actually received the decoration because he worked for the United States Government. At that time medals and decorations issued by another government could not be accepted by persons working in the Civil Service. The medal, consequently, was accepted on his behalf and held in custody by the U.S. State Department until such time as he would retire from his official position with the government.

As he was now officially retiring and the State Department would release the decoration, Mr. Werner mentioned how nice it would be if the medal could be presented to him by the Belgian ambassador, for that would make it so much more official.

I agreed and contacted my friend, His Excellency Baron van Scheyven, the ambassador from Belgium, and asked him if he would have a little presentation ceremony.

To my great delight the Baron consented. Not only did he agree to present the decoration to Mr. Werner personally, but he would also arrange a reception at the Embassy in his honor. Tuesday afternoon, September 12, 1967, was the designated date.

Thirty-one years had passed since King Albert had bestowed the award, but Belgium had not forgotten Victor Werner.

Washington is beautiful in the fall. The smoldering heat that envelops the city in summer has turned to a gentle warmth occasionally interrupted by a burst of crisp fresh air. Every day more leaves change to vibrant autumn colors harmonizing with the season, and flocks of little white clouds appear in the azure-blue sky to make the spectacle more breath-taking.

September 12 was just such a day.

The ambassador's invitation was for a reception at four o'clock.

When we entered the Embassy's exquisite drawing room, we were moved by its beauty and elegance. The high-ceilinged room—palatial, yet inviting—was decorated at one end with French period pieces in muted blue, ornamented by a huge vase overflowing with blue and purple flowers. The other end of the room was similar, but in palest gold, graced by another striking floral bouquet of yellow and white.

We learned that all decorating at the Embassy was personally planned and supervised by Baroness van Scheyven.

By experience I know that embassy receptions are quite similar. There are a few speeches, a few kind remarks, and a round of toasting the distinguished visitors. This one was to be highlighted by the official presentation of the Silver Medal of Leopold II, a toast to Mr. Werner, and then it would be over. Yet I sensed that this occasion would be different. How and in what manner I did not quite know, yet the feeling persisted.

As the decoration was given for the humanitarian deeds performed by Mr. Werner during World War I, much of the conversation preceding the actual ceremony related to that war. Guests were reminiscing and sharing their experiences of how the war had affected their lives in different parts of the world.

My eyes roamed along the ceiling of that elegantly appointed room, down the wall, until I was looking through the open terrace doors watching the clouds nudge each other, gently, delicately . . .

Then it happened! Just as Baron van Scheyven began the presentation, a small dove appeared, flying under the terrace awning and through the doors into the drawing room. With a soft fluttering of wings he circled the room.

My heart smiled.

"Oh, Mr. Ambassador," I cried happily, "how fortunate! This is a good omen—a special sign! It signifies something of tremendous international importance."

By now the guests were watching the dove. He circled the room once more, alighting on a magnificent crystal chandelier, one of a pair adorning the room.

The ambassador became slightly flustered and called for both his secretary and butler. Sensing that he would attempt to remove the dove, I interrupted.

"Oh, please do not, Mr. Ambassador," I pleaded. "You do not realize how much the appearance of this dove means! Just leave him there, please . . . please! But"—and here my feminine instincts took precedence over my psychic instincts —"you might want to place a newspaper under the chandelier . . . just in case—your Aubusson is so rare and beautiful."

A ripple of laughter broke out at the very thought of such

an unassuming visitor misbehaving in such dignified sur-
roundings.

The ambassador, however, saw the humor of the situation
and asked his secretary with a hint of political wit:

"Bring me a copy of the ———." He named a particular
newspaper. "It might serve a good purpose for once!"

He turned to me, gesturing apologetically.

"I am sorry, Mrs. Dixon. This is the first time anything
like this has ever happened. In the eight years that we have
lived here these doors have been opened many times before,
but never has a bird of any kind flown into the Embassy
. . . please believe me!"

I did not question it then, for I felt God had sent this dove
for a specific purpose.

Baron van Scheyven walked toward his secretary who had
returned with the newspaper. Now everyone became an expert in strategy, and with advice from all the guests as to its
most beneficial position, the paper soon covered the Aubusson
—directly beneath the branch of sparkling crystal on which
the dove was perched.

The rug shielded, the ambassador tried to put an end to
the incident with a casual remark.

"There is one law we all have to take into consideration,"
he said, glancing upward with a slight frown, "and that is
the law of gravity."

Throughout all the commotion Victor Werner had been
momentarily neglected, but the ceremony more than com-
pensated.

"It is my privilege to have you here," the ambassador
started the ceremony, "and to be able to bestow upon you,
Mr. Werner, the Silver Medal of the Order of Leopold, an
outstanding decoration for services extended to my country.
My King, my Government, and I wholeheartedly give you,
Victor Werner, this token of our esteem and appreciation."

He took the impressive medal and carefully pinned it on
Victor's lapel. "I am sorry you had to wait so long," he con-

cluded, "but I am truly honored to be the one to present this medal to you."

Tears of happiness welled up in Mr. Werner's eyes as he thanked the ambassador. Everyone gathered around, congratulating him and admiring his medal.

With an almost imperceptible movement of his hand the ambassador motioned into the room two tall, handsome butlers, a youthful brunet and a silver-haired major-domo, bearing trays of champagne and dainty biscuits.

"Let's enjoy the terrace," the ambassador suggested, strolling toward the open doors. One by one the guests followed, forming small groups.

Suddenly Jimmy called our attention back to the dove.

"Look!" he exclaimed. "Look at the dove . . . he seems to be following us."

Quickly I turned and, reentering the drawing room, spoke to the little dove in soft, caressing tones.

"Come here, little one," I coaxed. "Come and let me hold you."

Just as though he understood my words, he circled around again and flew directly to me, touching down gently on my outstretched right hand.

With the dove in the palm of my hand I slowly turned and walked back onto the terrace, talking to him softly.

The dove's unusual response to me attracted everyone's attention. All conversation ceased; every eye was on us, aware that something was happening beyond what they were seeing.

The dove nestled in my hand and watched my face intently as if afraid of missing one single word. His tiny black eyes never wavered but kept looking at me with great serenity.

Was he telling me something? I was not sure, but I stopped talking nevertheless and tried to concentrate with him on whatever his coming was meant to convey.

God reveals Himself and His plans in many ways, and when He sets the stage, no power or person can stop Him!

My mind's eye can often look deep into the far beyond, and my mind's ear can sometimes tune in to the far sounds of heaven, but this time I not only saw and heard, but *felt*—God omnipresent, God controlling and God directing every capsule of time and space. Gone from my consciousness was the reception, gone were the people and Victor Werner. I was alone with the Eternal One, and felt reverently awed, and was experiencing again that beautiful unearthly quiet in the vast unending space of the great beyond.

Hardly conscious of moving, I stepped onto the terrace, the dove in my hand. People moved a little, off to one side, and to me it seemed as if the Red Sea were parting again.

Visions came to me . . . scenes of what would be.

It was as if I were not me—a mortal—any more, but a spirit of consciousness—off somewhere in vast, unbounded space, looking down the years at things to come.

I could feel the earth shake and tremble underfoot. Then it seemed as though the world had stopped rotating on its axis. I saw that in this century there will be many geological and geographical changes and many earthquakes . . . rivers will cease to flow, and others will alter their courses. Where water is now, there will be land, and where there is land today, wild, swirling water will rush in and destroy everything in its path.

It was then that I saw the blazing Cross appear in the eastern skies high over a dark and lonely hill. It was great and magnificent . . . ominous and foreboding, yet so majestic and full of love that I knew it was the Cross of Christ!

Waves of thunder and lightning rolled in succession until all creation seemed to be echoing the same sound that enveloped the earth when He created it. And then there was silence . . . and suddenly I felt no longer alone. All sound had retreated into the great void, and instead peace and tranquillity covered the devastated earth.

Everyone in the world was somehow seeing the Cross with me! And it came to me that everyone witnessing this spectacle understood clearly that it was the illuminating Light of God within themselves!

They knew, as did I, that we no longer needed "the moon or stars by night, or sun to shine by day"—each one of us was experiencing the spiritual glory of the Light of God within.

And the world, and all its peoples, stood still.

Entranced, I started to raise the dove up and let him go, but Someone guided my hand down again, and as it came to rest I heard the voice of our Lord Jesus say, "Now you are ALL my disciples!"

I heard—and hearing I *knew*—for He made His meaning clear beyond question—that the day will come when religions as we know them today, Christian, Jew, Hindu, Buddhist, will be no more, and we will all indeed be true disciples of Jesus.

And with this flash of perfect understanding came His compassionate voice again:

"Now you are all my disciples!"

I kept listening, but the voice had retracted its soft-sounding echoes and was gone.

Once again I was mortal. All sights and sounds had retreated into the great beyond.

My hand rose up into the air, to bid the dove farewell.

He slowly positioned himself in my hand and, his message delivered, without a backward glance he spread his soft feathered wings and flew westward into the setting sun.

The vision had ended.

When later I told my friend John Fetzer about it, he became extremely silent and thoughtful. John, president of the Detroit Tigers baseball club and president of a chain of radio and television stations in Michigan and Nebraska, is unquestionably a most realistic businessman. Yet—and this only increases his stature as a man—he has never allowed his realistic attitude to blind him to the spiritual core of life or phenomena of the psychic world. I have heard people refer to John as an "abstract intellectual," and though I do not share this view entirely, he is nevertheless a deep thinker.

John is convinced that the appearance of the dove and the ensuing vision were a true manifestation from above.

"I seriously suspect that the coming of the dove," he commented after giving it some intense thought, "and your subsequent contact with the Messenger of Peace, has a connotation that should bring home a very valuable lesson, not only to the hierarchy of the United States, but to the average person as well. Doves, of course, have always been associated with peace. There is abundant literature on the subject to substantiate this.

"It would be my feeling that, since you are particularly endowed with bringing messages to people in high places who deal with the instrumentalities of war and the many hazards in which the United States of America finds itself, it is appropriate, indeed, that you should receive a message that would alert us to make every effort to arrive at peaceful solutions to the world's problems instead of resorting to armed conflict. It seems to me that if our country continues to pursue its present course it could very well lead not only to our own destruction but to that of the entire world, which would set back our evolutionary development literally thousands of years.

"The fact that you participated in this message of peace brought by a dove appearing from nowhere and departing into a vacuum of mystery would indicate to me that the message originated from the same Source that gives you the talent to foresee coming world events."

There are times now when, in the twilight of the evening, I recall those treasured moments when the voice of Our Lord Jesus prophesied that we would someday be "all one under God."

Much has been prophesied for the years following 1999 when this vision will become a reality . . . and much will happen before that day. Yet I believe that the sounding of that voice heralded a new era of understanding, of love and devotion, for the sign of the dove is the sign of God's continuing love and plans for all of us.

3

God Speaks to Men

It was when the little dove came to rest on my outstretched hand that I was reminded once more how close we are to recognizing that we are all one under God. Eventually His will shall become our way.

Since God creates us one by one, His loving eye is on each one of us as it is on the sparrow. He is continually speaking to us and we can hear Him if we will open our minds and hearts to listen. He wants to use each one of us as a means of bringing about His Kingdom on earth. He wants us to be channels through which His Divine Plan is made known and fulfilled.

It is an awesome and inspiring feeling to be a worker for the Lord. . . .

I know this feeling because I have known its joys since my childhood.

It began in an unusual way when a gentle gypsy lady called my mother's attention to the unique line patterns in my hands.

In fascination she pointed to the inside of my right hand and exclaimed, "She's got the Star of David in her hand, and here"—she gasped and took a second look—"here's the Half Moon!"

My mother smiled understandingly, for somehow she seemed to feel the significance of it all.

The gypsy woman continued, "Your child, madam, is destined for great things. In both her hands she has all the markings of a great mystic."

Lost in deep thought, she turned around and disappeared into her wagon. When she returned she had a ball in her hand—a crystal ball.

"Here, my little one," she said softly, placing the ball gently into my outstretched hands. "Take it—tell me what you see."

I looked into it and what I saw was so beautiful it almost made me cry. I saw a wild, rocky coast in a far-off land and a turbulent sea crashing into the jagged edges of the crumbling rocks. Giant waves split into a shower of tiny droplets of white foamy rain, drifting down and up again, losing themselves on the whisper of the wind. Farther inland, a sea gull aimed for the clouds, flying to fulfillment of his destiny.

"You are describing my homeland, little one," the gypsy said sadly. "You've just seen the most wonderful sight on earth. Keep the ball. It is yours. It can do more in your hands than in mine!"

It was my first encounter with a gypsy, and through that experience I began to realize that I had a specific purpose in life.

To know that one is called by God for a special purpose is a knowledge that cannot be compared to anything else. People have often asked me how I *know* that what I receive psychically will come true. The answer is: my predictions do *not* always come true.

There are many different ways in which the future is revealed to me, and only a limited number of these events are made known to me through revelation.

Revelations are signs of the will of God, and not the will of man. When *God* reveals a future event through a revelation, nothing man can do will change it. The Lord gives a revelation to anyone whom He chooses, when He chooses, and how He chooses. A revelation has nothing whatsoever to do with extrasensory perception. It is God revealing His will, and when He chooses to use me as a channel for His revelation, I listen, I see, and I feel . . .

Another but a less certain way through which I receive knowledge of future events is what I call the "psychic way." Often when I meet people and shake their hands, I feel vibrations. By sensing and interpreting these vibrations, I can tell many things about that person. I "see" even more if I have a chance to *touch* their hands with the tip of the ring finger of my right hand. My fingers are supersensitive, and many times a gentle touch enables me to pick up an individual channel of communication with eternity. When I say "channel," I mean a communications frequency that has been given to us by our Creator. We all have our own individual channels, our own frequencies, for communication with the Lord. Often I can pick up an individual's "channel" as soon as I meet him, for sometimes this signal is so strong that it penetrates whatever disturbance there might be. Interestingly enough, I have never yet encountered two people who communicate on the same "channel." I have no doubt that most people are not aware of their own "channels," but to me these signals are so clear and unmistakably real that they often reveal to me what happened to them at an early age as well as what will happen to them until their last day on earth.

Another way of receiving the signals is through a direct contact with the Lord. When I pray and meditate and ask the Lord for guidance, many things are revealed to me, because it is at those moments of quiet contact with God that I become aware of the many signals surrounding us. It is at those moments that many "events-in-the-making" seem to close in on me. Somehow I keep getting extremely strong signals from Russia. They, the Russians, have their own aims in life, but they concentrate on their worldly desires and not on God's desires for them. They are filled with their own planning, their own thinking, and their own ideas.

The next strongest signals I have received up to now have

always been connected with the Kennedy family. They seem to have a strong purpose, too, and that strength of thought is powerful.

Many times when I need an answer to a specific question, I meditate with that one question in mind, knowing that if I concentrate, meditate, and pray, God will reveal the answer to me. It is almost like hearing the wind blowing and howling around your house on a stormy autumn night—the stronger the wind, the more clearly you can hear its sound. Often the answer to my question is already being worked out in other people's minds, but I am not aware of it until God allows me to "tune in" on their frequencies. This enables me to pick up their thoughts and conversations without being present.

Telepathy is still another way. Of course, many people talk without having anything on their minds, but the *thinking* people's thoughts are easy to read. Just being near them often betrays their innermost secrets. The crystal ball I use is somewhat of an extension of this telepathic ability. The ball is not in itself a power but a point of concentration—an instrument. When I ask someone to look into it and concentrate, I am able to see not only their innermost thoughts, but also become aware of what is going on in their subconscious minds and their personal hopes and plans. I see things that have been there for years without their knowing it.

Dreams are *still* another way.

Both the Old and the New Testaments speak of dreams. So does history, and so does literature.

In Numbers 12:6, the Old Testament tells us:

"And He said, Hear now my words: If there be a prophet among you, I the Lord will make myself known unto him in a vision, and will speak unto him in a dream."

In the New Testament we read:

"And when they were come into the house, they saw the young child with Mary, his mother, and fell down, and wor-

shipped him: and when they had opened their treasures, they
presented unto him gifts; gold, frankincense and myrrh.

"And being warned of God in a dream that they should
not return to Herod, they departed into their own country
another way.

"And when they were departed, behold, the angel of the
Lord appeared to Joseph in a dream, saying, Arise, and take
the young child and his mother, and flee into Egypt, and be
thou there until I bring thee word: for Herod will seek the
young child to destroy him."

Many years ago when the Church of St. John Lateran was
the seat of the Church of Rome, Pope Innocent III dreamed
he saw a little man bracing himself against St. John Lateran,
which was tilting to one side. Interpreting this to mean the
structure of the church was weakening, he wondered long
and often about the identity of this strange little man.

In the course of time St. Francis and his first followers
sought an audience with the Pope. Pope Innocent, at once
recognizing him as the little man who had appeared to him
in the dream, listened intently to all he had to say and ac-
tivated many of the ideas advocated by St. Francis.

It was because of dreams that Sigmund Freud, the Austrian
physician and psychologist, founded his famous school of
psychoanalysis.

In my own experiences God often reveals things to me
when I am on the threshold of awakening from a sound sleep.

Although there is little or no doubt that dreams at times
reveal our innermost thoughts, the complexities and emotions of our everyday lives often make it unwise for us to
attempt to analyze our dreams unless we know how to interpret them.

In my case God often uses dreams to warn me of events
to come, or to give me special guidance in this oldest method
of communication between God and man.

When asleep, your conscious mind is at rest, and the subconscious mind is very vulnerable to anything that comes

within mental reach. It may be the Lord's spirit that wants to communicate with you, or the devil who wants to entice you, using the medium of the unconscious mind.

I firmly believe that the subconscious mind will take over and continue working on the channel you use during your waking hours. In other words, if the conscious mind operates on a sinful channel, the subconscious will stay on that channel, opening up the mind for Satan's influence. This is why it is so important to keep your channel tuned directly to the Creator during your waking hours. When the end of the day approaches, take inventory of your thoughts, and ask God for forgiveness, thereby closing the door to the influence of Satan on your subconscious mind. You can rest assured that God will not allow Satan to use the channel you have reserved for exclusive contact with Him.

To me, a revelation is God's hand resting on me, revealing what is to take place, and it is an experience that is completely different.

A revelation is something special. Sometimes two, three, or even four years may go by without God granting me a revelation, and then some morning I wake up and feel just wonderful. I feel inspired and know that something great is going to happen. I feel as though I am engulfed in love and feel like embracing life itself, and say, "Oh, God, it is wonderful to be alive!" I feel inspired, and the whole day seems to be different. No one can get me into an argument, and no problem seems too big to be solved. When I go home at night, I have that spring in my walk that I do not usually have, and the next day this feeling of greatness and peace multiplies. The third day it becomes as big as a mountain, and then in the evening of the third day I know that God has taken these three days to prepare me for His message, for a revelation always follows on the fourth day. Some time during that day God will reveal His wisdom to me and show me His will for a given situation. All of my revelations deal with international situations. They are never intended for one person as an individual.

During the remainder of the fourth day, after a revelation has been given me, my love for humanity is so great that I feel like touching people to let them *share* it and let them *feel* how great and wonderful God's love really is. Believe me, this is an experience that money cannot buy. It is an experience that happens only after one has been prepared by the Lord for a revelation.

Whatever God reveals in these revelations must come to pass. These are not man-made plans; they are either the will of God or God allows them to happen. In the case of the assassination of President John Kennedy, the knowledge of his death came to me in a revelation, and there was nothing I could do to stop the murder. God alone is great enough to bring good out of what appears to us to be tragic and evil at times. Those who believe in the power and goodness of God accept His will. The will of humanity cannot change the will of God.

The deaths of Dr. Martin Luther King, Jr., and Senator Robert F. Kennedy were given me through telepathy, not through a revelation, and need not have taken place if the events surrounding these two people had been altered.

After a revelation has been given to me on the fourth day, God's great love still surrounds me and stays with me for another three days—for a period of seven days in all, and then on the eighth day it is all over. Sometimes after a revelation I think, "Oh, will it ever be possible to re-create these glorious seven days?" But I know that a thought like this is in vain, for God put that wonderful feeling as a protective shield around me to prepare me for the coming of the revelation, and nothing I can do will ever bring it back.

During these seven days I become so sensitive and receptive that I tune in on signals from people I have never heard of and receive information I did not know existed. The slightest human brain wave becomes a powerful beacon, and

I know without wanting to what the people around me are thinking; but I know, too, that I can affect their thought patterns by touching them and in so doing bring a bit of God's love into their lives. It is not something which is mine that I transmit to them; it is rather a special gift that the Lord transmits to them through me.

I know He is Love. I work very hard and try to base my entire life on bringing this realization to those with whom I come in contact. I try, but I do not always succeed. I live each day with the hope of doing better . . . with the help of God.

4

The Future That Was

The rare and beautiful experiences of divine revelation are moments of special gifts. Each of us, however, lives each day with special gifts which are a part of our very being, and life is a process of discovering and developing these God-given gifts within each one of us.

I have been given certain psychic gifts which I have been working to develop and use in accordance with God's will as I am able to understand His will—*His purpose for my life.*

There are many ways in which I have discovered and have been able gradually through the years to develop my ability, my talent, to perceive the abilities and the potential in the talent of others, to receive the thoughts and man-made plans of others, and, at times, to "see" the outcome of certain man-made events.

One of my early experiences was connected with a crystal ball. It occurred when, at eight years of age, I "read" for Elinor Glyn, while she was in California for the filming of her famous *Three Weeks*.

"I see you," I told her, "writing by the light of the moon . . . I see you gathering words and balancing them delicately before you use them . . . that is the time when you have your greatest inspiration, is it not?"

She looked up and nodded. She grabbed my hand and

held it tightly, and for a fleeting moment we were very, very close.

I remember thinking how beautiful Elinor Glyn really was and felt a deep sympathy for her. It was not her fame that attracted me but her face and personality.

I guess I have always gravitated to older people. I fondly remember my early years when, as soon as I heard visitors downstairs, I would jump out of bed and peek around the corner in my nightclothes.

When my parents were entertaining I was permitted to get out of bed—not that they encouraged it; they tolerated it. Many times I ran down and jumped onto my father's knee. Sitting there, safe and secure within the protective warmth of his arms, I would tell my parents' friends all about themselves. They loved it, of course, but whether they understood my mission in life is something I will never know.

Perhaps I grew up too fast in those early years. I never played with dolls; in fact, I did not even miss them! I know some girls would feel deprived if they didn't have dolls to play with, but I did not feel that way at all. To me the most fascinating part of life was the future.

I had that crystal ball for many years until one night when I returned to our Washington apartment and realized as I began to unlock the door that someone had broken into it during my absence. I went from room to room. Closets had been searched, drawers had been upturned, yet nothing seemed to be missing until I looked for the crystal ball.

It was the only item stolen that night.

The ball I now have was given to me in appreciation by a woman who had met me years before the theft. I was not enthusiastic at all about having to meet her, but my friend, Lady Bumgardner, insisted that I see her.

"Do me a favor, Jeane dear. Please try to find a few moments to listen to her."

Lady, to me, is a saint on this earth . . . I could not refuse her.

But it was one of those hectic days when everything seemed to demand my attention and I just could not see her then. I told Lady so.

Her friend's insistence, however, was stronger than my objections, and when my secretary came into the office the next morning telling me that a close friend of Lady Bumgardner's would like to see me for a moment, I had to give in. I try to be sensitive to people's troubles no matter how or when they come to me, and when I greeted her and touched her fingers, I knew she was extremely upset. Just imagine your fingers having been sanded down to the raw nerve; it makes you feel the slightest things, even a speck of dust. That was the way I sensed her problems.

The crystal ball was in my office that day, and I offered to use it to look into her problems for her. Now I do want to emphasize that when I use a crystal ball, much of what I observe is transmitted to me through telepathy, so in reality you might say that all I do is pick up thoughts and vibrations from the individual that is with me. The ball serves as a means of concentration.

Within minutes I knew that this woman was planning to go to Europe and divorce her husband.

"Don't get this divorce," I pleaded with her. "Your life means too much to take a step like that. Stay with your husband, for within six months your entire life will change. You'll imagine yourself living in another world before long —the change will be that great!"

She postponed the divorce, and I had almost put the entire matter out of my mind when, two days before the end of the six months' period, she called me from Washington's Union Station, informing me that her husband had died and that she was taking his body to Cleveland for burial.

"Please let me see you once more," she begged. "There's so much I want to talk to you about . . ."

When we met, she didn't wait a moment to tell me what was on her mind.

"This time I am not going back home," she blurted out. "I can't get along with my sister-in-law, and my husband's inheritance is more than enough to keep me free from worry for years to come."

Suddenly it came to me—the answer she needed.

"Go back—your sister-in-law is not well. Go back and look after her. She needs you."

Was it compassion? I will never know, but for whatever reason she went home. Her sister-in-law died two months later, rewarding her for her devotion with a sizable inheritance.

I relate this because when my crystal ball was stolen, it was this woman who called me and asked if I would let her get another one for me. She commissioned an agent to organize a search throughout the world, trying to find a crystal ball that would at least equal the one I had just lost.

Christmas is always a time of happiness and meditation, and Christmas, 1962, was no exception. I was spending a part of the holiday season with her at her villa in Rome when she received word that a crystal ball fitting my specifications had been found.

"A Belgian jeweler has one and claims it possesses great magnetic power and says it once belonged to a Belgian nobleman. He wants to send it over right away. Would you like him to do that?"

"Of course!"

A contessa arrived early the next morning with the crystal ball. It was perfect.

I don't use the crystal ball very often, yet each time I use it I seem to "see" something dramatically significant.

This was the case when, in May 1965, I concentrated on Europe and was startled to see two objects obviously of Russian origin, one of which was bearing the strange initials MIRV, orbiting the earth in a path which appeared as a blue belt. The significance of the other one was not revealed to me until Christmas of 1966. It was a multi-test vehicle, testing a propulsion system using cosmic rays and magnetic forces. I saw these forces attracting and repelling themselves in a way which would harness them to drive a spaceship into outer space. The Russians are far ahead of us in this field, and we must catch up or be left behind in interplanetary travel. I know now why the importance of the MIRV was shown to me before the test vehicle was revealed, because the MIRV was and still is an immediate threat to our survival.

"It looks like an atomic-missile-firing submarine," I recall describing it to myself—then I realized it was an earth-orbiting missile carrier, capable of firing atomic missiles through its torpedo-like tubes.

I looked again and noticed separate electronic guidance systems in each of the missiles, enabling it to seek out its own target.

More than two years ago I warned the Administration of this threat. Unfortunately, our Secretary of Defense did not respond. However, if the Department of Defense had taken the time to insert the probability of such development into the calculating mechanical brain of the computer, we might now be ahead of the Russians instead of frantically trying to "catch up" with them.

In 1965 I described the MIRV as a "submarine of the sky" because of its resemblance to a missile-firing submarine. Dr. John S. Foster, Director of Defense Research and Engineering in Dallas, described it as a "space bus" in a speech given two years later on December 13, 1967.

In 1965 I warned that nine of our great eastern cities were in danger. Warheads are placed in the Soviet MIRV satellites in multiples of three. The first contained nine warheads— targeted for nine cities . . .

On October 7, 1967, before the Norfolk Chamber of Commerce, Norfolk, Virginia, I pointed out that "until June 1, 1967, I did not know what the letters MIRV stood for. I only knew it meant danger to us." The June issue of *Fortune* magazine published an article entitled "The Shifting Equation

of Nuclear Defense" by Richard J. Whalen. In this article
Mr. Whalen discussed the value of the MIRV's.

Later in that same year Mr. Robert McNamara, our then
Secretary of Defense, admitted on the eve of the fiftieth
anniversary of the Russian Revolution that the U.S.S.R. was
now *producing* a MIRV . . . *this, two and one-half years
after my initial warning!*

(The *Fortune* magazine story also touched on another one
of my predictions. In 1963, while appearing on the Johnny
Carson "Tonight" show, I warned that "a burst over our heads
could and would put out some of the lights and would
neutralize our communications." *Two years later, the great
New England blackout occurred,* and for the first time
Johnny Carson's studio was paralyzed—the lights were out!)

The Soviets have defensive missiles "creating sunlike energy bursts and dispersing enormous pulses of thermal radiation in the near vacuum of space," *Fortune* reported, and
continuing his commentary on the Russian test program, Mr.
Whalen went on to state that "the Soviet tests clearly had
been planned years in advance. Among their seventy-one
shots were proof tests, weapon-systems tests, effects, and tests
with missiles and radar. The Russians, obviously extending
their anti-ballistic missile technology, on two occasions during the tests launched an ICBM, intercepted it with a nuclear
blast, and then fired a *second* missile, presumably to determine
whether its warhead was affected by the radiation resulting
from the prior explosion. They also studied the blackout
effects of the blasts on their radar."

*I saw this test years ago, and this was the reason I warned
against the Test Ban Treaty. Mr. Whalen was correct in his
article, but he left out one important detail. I saw three large
missiles fired in sequence. The first two were 200 miles apart,
the third, 500 miles behind the second. The first missile burst
in an atomic blast. The second passed through the mushroom
cloud . . . then an intercept missile came up from the ground
to destroy the third missile.*

The first was a preliminary test. When corrections were made and, as explained by scientists, "the circuits were 'hardened' against radiation and fission," the Soviets tried a second test much similar to the first one. This one was highly successful, and as a direct result of this well-planned test program, they proceeded without delay with the construction of their anti-ballistic missile defense.

Knowing what was happening in the Soviet Union, I called two powerful senators during the summer of 1967 and begged them not to ratify the "Consular Treaty" with Russia on the basis of the Administration's warning that we needed observers in the "Tallinn corridor." I did not know at that time what the "Tallinn corridor" was, but both Generals Bernard Schriever and Curtis LeMay have since stated that Tallinn-type installations are missiles and anti-ballistic missiles capable of producing x-rays let loose by ultrahigh-energy nuclear explosions. These "pulsed" x-rays can cause violent reactions within the molecular structure of materials and can destroy or neutralize attacking nuclear missiles.

In 1965, the Administration would not take time to investigate my warnings seriously. After having done some extensive research into this matter, Mr. Whalen admitted in the same *Fortune* magazine article that "the U. S. takes the x-ray threat from the Soviet ABM defenses seriously enough to be engaged in costly modification of missiles whose components are vulnerable. For example, the fine gold wires (which readily absorb x-rays) are being replaced in the guidance computer circuitry of the Minuteman II, and the change is being incorporated into the design of the Poseidan and Minuteman III. Because reflective coatings used to protect a missile nose cone from the heat of re-entry are ineffective against thermal x-rays, new hardening techniques and shielding materials are being sought."

However, until we actually test against a super 100-megaton bomb as the Soviets did, we will not be sure. Also a substitute has to be found for the gold contact points on an atomic war-

*head because in a mental picture, a psychic vision, I saw
flashes going through the gold points, neutralizing the bomb.
We should immediately begin with a crash program to exploit
the power to be found in cosmic rays and magnetic forces.
If we fail in this, we may still lose our leadership in space
exploration.*

When reporting what I see psychically, I am, as I should
be, as impersonal about it as I can be. Often I do not have
the slightest understanding of what I see; yet the fragments
fall into place when the predicted events come to pass. It is
like watching the face of a clock. I can see the hands move
yet do not know the workings of the mechanism behind it.
In the case of a prophecy, however, there is a divine power
at work. Let me say this: I have no pact with God that He
will show me everything—but I am eternally grateful for what
He has allowed me to see.

When people ask me to describe my gift, I am at a loss.
They may just as well ask me to describe love or electricity.
Sometimes I get things so fleetingly that, intent upon understanding what I am seeing, I fail to concentrate on the fine
points. Consequently, unless I have someone beside me to
whom I can describe my vision and the various details, much
of it may get lost. My knowledge about the Russian test
programs, for example, did not come to me in a revelation,
but in a psychic vision—very possibly through thought transference. Sometimes I become so ultrasensitive that many
channels of communication seem to open up all at the same
time, exposing hitherto secret man-made plans.

A typical experience began to take shape when I first met
Jean Stout, wife of a retired Navy commander who, at that
time (September 1965), had become Chief, Mission Opera-
tions, of the Office of Manned Space Flight. In this function
he was directly involved in the Apollo space program.

Jean Stout and I met in our real estate office in Washington, but what started out as a business meeting soon developed into a sharing of mutual interests. Business moved into

the background while we explored each other's personalities. We both liked what we saw, for our friendship has continued to grow ever since.

It was while on a speaking engagement in Cleveland in September 1965 that I placed a phone call to Jean Stout because a rather puzzling series of what seemed to be highly technical terms dealing with space flight had just come to me. My first impression was, "These are intended for Fred Stout," and I told this to Jean.

"Please write down what I am going to tell you," I told her. "The words and pictures I will describe make no sense to me whatsoever, but I will give them to you just as I have received them. I am sure they are of great importance to your husband, and I felt that I just had to call you!

"Tell your husband that he will be involved in selecting the 'window' for the first manned lunar firings. Don't get too excited about this as yet though, for it is at least three years off. He may, however, be interested to know that I see him watching—over an eighty-three-hour span—what appears to be a unit made up of two television sets. There is also some sort of a slide arrangement, looking like a red-hot triangle, that moves up and down.

"Tell Fred. He'll want to know this!"

Fred Stout was stunned when Jean confronted him with the information later on in the day.

"This is incredible," the startled Navy commander replied. "This is just plain weird. How can she know about this?"

"What is this 'window' that Jeane Dixon referred to?" Jean Stout asked.

"It is a term commonly used in space terminology to describe the period of time during which we can launch a space craft. Determining the 'window' involves taking many factors into consideration. Some of these are earth rotation, launch and recovery times and areas, and sufficient daylight in the launch area to permit defueling in the event of a scrub.

"In the case of a direct lunar shot, the 'window' becomes

even more intricate since we will have to consider conditions in the target areas as well as those of earth."

"What about the 'slide' and the two television sets?" Jean asked.

"That's a pretty accurate description of a space capsule's reentry pattern," he continued. "The thing which looks like a glowing triangle signifies the module which must follow the graded slide when moving back into our atmosphere or else either burn up from too great a reentry velocity or get out of control due to lack of speed. While the actual movement of the capsule within the triangle is, of course, handled by the astronauts themselves, the entire reentry process is controlled by a man standing behind a console, equipped with two television screens . . ."

For many months thereafter Jean Stout and I kept in close contact with each other. I always looked forward to seeing her and enjoyed our times together. Her brilliant mind and gift of total recall has always been a source of inspiration and fascination to me.

But there was nothing enjoyable or inspirational about what happened when we lunched together at the Mayflower Hotel in Washington on December 20, 1966, when Jean asked me to meditate on the future of the space program.

"I am interested in the Apollo program. How does it look?"

I held out my hand to her.

"You have something in your purse that has to do with the Apollo," I countered. "May I have a look at it?"

Jean opened her purse.

"Is this it?" she questioned while showing me a memo pad on which was a sticker seal of the Apollo.

"No. It is something cubicle . . ."

Jean was perplexed, but searching further, she found a little gold plastic cube that held an Apollo tie tack which Fred had brought back with him from Cape Kennedy.

"Is this it?"

I nodded.

"But how in the world could you know I had that thing?" she exclaimed, somewhat puzzled. "Fred got it only yesterday and dropped it into my purse as we drove in this morning . . ."

I didn't answer but instead took the top off the tiny module and peeked inside. There they were—three miniature astronauts, reclining on their couches. I stared at them and felt a sudden wave of pity engulf me. Jean commented later on that she noticed a tremendous change come over me—as if I had suddenly discovered death in Paradise.

"Jean," I said softly, "there's death in this program . . ." Horror filled me as I watched what was unfolding before my eyes. "Jean, there is going to be a loss of life in this module before the end of January. Three men will die in the capsule, but not necessarily in flight. What is going to happen will happen due to negligence. It can be avoided if the wiring is checked and rechecked and carefully examined. There is nothing, however, that your husband can do about it.

"There's also something strange about the floor of that capsule," I went on. "It seems so thin that it almost resembles tinfoil. I am afraid that a tool dropped on it or a heel pushed firmly against it would go right through it.

"And under the floor"—for a moment I stopped, groping for the right words—"under the floor I see a great clump of tangled wires . . ."

I took another close look at the capsule.

"I see a terrible fiery catastrophe . . . and it will cause the astronauts' deaths . . . I sense their souls leaving the blazing capsule in puffs of smoke . . ."

Both of us were shaken, and when Jean Stout put the capsule with the three little men back in her purse, it was as if she reverently put the men to rest.

We parted quietly, each with her own thoughts of the impending disaster.

Since Fred Stout had flown back to Cape Kennedy, Jean had arranged to meet two friends of hers and ride home with them. Discussing what I had told her, they advised Jean not to tell her husband inasmuch as he wouldn't take it seriously anyway.

When, however, Fred arrived at the airport just prior to the Christmas holidays, Jean did tell him anyway and his response was just about what she had expected.

"You sure have a collection of astonishing friends, honey," he remarked humorously. "We're not having a flight that soon, so you'd just as well forget about her prediction."

"But Jeane Dixon didn't say it would happen in *flight*," she emphasized. "She just said it would happen! And there's something else I want to tell you too—Jeane said something about the floor of the space capsule, something about it being very much like tinfoil and that a man could almost put his foot through it . . ."

Fred registered distinct surprise and after a mystified pause made some comment under his breath about some space designs being different—very different.

Then in the following month, on January 27, 1967, it happened! An uncontrollable blaze charred three promising young astronauts beyond recognition while they were testing the Apollo capsule on Cape Kennedy, leaving a stunned America in a state of shock.

I called Jean the morning after the tragedy and told her to tell Fred that he should have someone examine the wiring in the capsule as soon as it had cooled off sufficiently, and that he would find it would seem to be all wrong.

Later on that same day I called again and said that I had a strong impression that something like a screwdriver or wrench would be found at the trouble site. I don't know the first thing about the intricacies of electronic circuitry but could have drawn a diagram of the capsule's wiring system if I had been requested to do so, for by this time I knew the inside of the capsule as well as the designers.

Months later the final official report released to the public was supported by a photograph of a tool clumped in a maze of wires. . . .

After the tragedy Jean Stout left some pictures with me which related to the astronauts and the Apollo program. She felt, she said, that my husband might like to see them. As it turned out, they enabled me to visualize the astronauts on their couches and where they were found after the blaze had been extinguished.

In my psychic visions I often see words and terms that are not only completely unknown to me but seem to have a unique meaning to the program or occasion for which they were intended. In the case of the Apollo, the words "window," "zero gravity environment," and "vox" reached me with exceptional clarity. They didn't mean much to me, yet they are familiar to all who work in the space program. Since then Fred Stout has told me that "vox" is a type of communication system used in the Apollo program, but one which has been very troublesome. It doesn't always happen this way. Sometimes a large number of words are lost before I have a chance to use them because, I suppose, of my unfamiliarity with them and my inability to translate them into everyday language. To the complete mystification of many language specialists, I often "get" words, data and descriptions far superior and much more accurate than any terms or phrases in common usage, words usually only known to a scholarly few.

A significant aspect of the prediction regarding the Apollo program was that the accident was specifically set to take place "before the end of January"; the whole psychic experience was a complete surprise to me—it was certainly not something I would have introduced at a pre-Christmas luncheon. The information I received was minutely detailed, both verbally and pictorially.

To each of us God gives particular gifts and talents. He has given me the gift of psychic perception which enables me to "see" patterns in individual lives and to detect some man-made plans of men and nations. At times He has blessed me with the experience of being a channel through which He has revealed a part of His Divine Plan.

What follows is a record of what I have perceived through psychic visions concerning the affairs of men and of nations.

5

Psychic Visions Turned Reality

To many people race riots are a rather unexpected development of the last few years. "The social conditions were not ripe for them until now," they say.

Because they were man-made, these riots and conditions could have been prevented. My first view of this dark shadow, which is covering most of the United States today, came when, as a little girl, I was at prayer in the Sacred Heart Cathedral on Hollywood's famous Sunset Boulevard. While meditating, I received a vision of black people walking over the rooftops of our government buildings, symbolizing, of course, a disrespect by some for the established authority. But I also saw them being given positions of importance long before they were ready for them by those who were trying to serve their own selfish purposes.

It was in 1948, when I was looking for something far removed from anything remotely resembling uncontrolled riots and seeking help for someone with whom I had lunched that day, that suddenly the crystal ball was filled with tumult.

I saw helmeted police and heavily armed soldiers leading and dragging sullen and belligerent men through angry crowds. I saw wounded men bleeding in the streets, and the night air was filled with the screaming of sirens of police cars, ambulances, and fire engines. Men and women, filled with greed, smashed windows and looted stores while police and soldiers watched.

The flames and violence spread like an uncontrollable fungus all over the nation. I saw Washington in flames . . . *Right then I knew that these riots, instigated by the organizational geniuses of the U.S.S.R. working behind the scenes, would continue into 1968 and beyond.* I warned the nation about it repeatedly and told Madeline Maloney, a close friend of President and Mrs. Truman, about it, but my warnings were ignored. If my warnings had been taken seriously at that time, 1968 would not have gone down in the pages of U.S. history as the bloody year that it turned out to be. In the future the riots will *not* be confined to the United States but will erupt all over the world.

I started the year 1968 full of good intentions, and one of my first good deeds was calling Jean and Fred Stout to wish them a good and prosperous new year.

"And by the way," I commented toward the end of our conversation, "President Johnson will withdraw from the presidential race."

"Health reasons?" Jean queried.

"No," I replied. "His health is good, but he is just going to quit!" Jean must have given it some real thought and discussed it with many of her friends who dropped in that day, for she called me bright and early the next morning.

"You've really done it this time." She grinned. "Many of my friends are willing to believe some of your predictions, but this one is going a little too far. You just don't kill Santa Claus."

Whether or not President Johnson was a "Santa Claus" who created too many aid programs can only be decided by the impartial judges of history.

On March 31 I was home trying to nurse the effects of a bad case of sinus trouble when at about ten to nine in the evening my phone rang. It was Jean Stout.

"Do you still stay with your prediction that the President will withdraw from the upcoming race?" she asked. "My husband still thinks this is your wildest prediction to date."

"Yes," I told her, "and what's more, he will be announcing it on the 'special' from the White House that is to start within the next ten minutes. I suppose that as a good American I ought to go downstairs and listen to him, but he's going to announce that he is withdrawing from the race, and I already know that. There have been times during the past two months when I was less certain of it, but he has made his final decision. It's definite now."

A short time later my phone rang again.

"You were right, Jeane. The President did announce he shall not be a candidate for the Presidency again. How on earth did you know?"

"Call it 'telepathy,' call it 'thought transference' if you'd like. I knew it because I was tuned in on the President's channel and 'read' the conflict that raged within him."

Many people did not believe me when, at the time of the Kennedy inauguration, I predicted that not only would Jacqueline Kennedy add much glamour and many stars to her husband's crown but would end up losing some stars in her crown.

"Impossible," many of my friends commented when I told them about it. "She is too grand a lady for that." Another friend, Rose Dickens, felt the same way. "How could anyone as sweet and lovely as Jacqueline Kennedy tarnish her crown?" she asked.

I wondered too. I was fascinated when Mrs. Kennedy redecorated the White House and displayed an uncanny interest in restoring the presidential mansion to its present splendor. She filled the White House with renewed elegance—and friends and enemies alike admired her for it.

Her dignity, her royal bearing, and her inspiring discipline during the mournful days following her husband's assassination caused France's President Charles de Gaulle to say, "She gave an example to the whole world of how to behave."

If anything was happening to her crown, it was just the opposite of what I had predicted, but when a short time after the President's death Jacqueline and her sister, Princess Lee Radziwill, appeared in public with Marlon Brando, many people who knew about my prediction contacted me.

"Is this her mistake?" they asked. "Is this going to affect her 'crown'?"

My constant denials became almost monotonous.

"No, this is not it," I kept telling them, and, "No, her mistake will come *after* she has moved to New York."

"How about the big house she just bought in Georgetown?" I was asked. "Does this not indicate that she is going to remain here?"

"Her reputation will suffer as the result of something that has to do with a book," I finally replied, having not the slightest premonition as to how a book would become involved in this. I had not heard of any specific books being written about Mrs. Kennedy, nor did I know of anyone planning to write a book. When it was announced, however, that William Manchester had been requested to write a book about the President's death, I knew that was it.

"It has finally happened, Rose," I said to my friend. "This book will bring about the mistake that will weaken her pedestal. And when the book was published, it did just that. In fact, it started during the final days preceding publication when a disagreement between the Kennedys on one side and William Manchester on the other resulted in a legal battle over who had the right to make the final changes in the manuscript. A nationwide survey indicated that, as a result of this controversy, one-third of the people polled had lost faith in Jacqueline Kennedy.

There is no doubt that she had a right—a *responsibility*— to object to anything in the book that would tend to invade the privacy of her own immediate family. The agreement she had drawn up with William Manchester specified just that. She had, in fact, the right to read the manuscript and make the changes herself. When it finally came to a reading of the manuscript, however, she delegated this responsibility to others and then complained to the publisher that not all corrections had been made prior to publication. She asked for further changes at the last moment. This caused such a furor that the items she wanted to delete from the manuscript were printed the world over, thus producing a hundred times more readership than they would have had otherwise.

Many of my visions seem to foretell the impossible—as was the case with the vision about Jacqueline Kennedy. Yet it came true. Another one that falls into the same category concerns the eventual return of Russia to Christianity.

For a long time now I have known that Russia is being made ready to undergo a tremendous change. It was made clear to me in a vision, however, that this development would take place in the distant future. The Russian altar I saw was far away, but I saw that, once again, the altar of Christian churches would be within the reach of the people of Russia. This religious revival will be a part of a general renaissance —a rebirth of faith in Jesus Christ.

I now see Stalin's daughter, Svetlana Alliluyeva, as a central figure in this development and as a major influence in the defection of many Communist officials to the West.

The vision about Svetlana Alliluyeva came to me in the early part of May 1967 as I was speaking in a Maryland church. Suddenly the faces of the congregation dimmed and I began to see a vision of Svetlana, who had just recently arrived in this country. The vision grew until she completely blotted out the entire congregation. Rays of sunshine surrounded her, and behind her I saw a steady stream of men and women slowly moving down the road of defection.

I knew from this vision that her defection to the West

would mean a turning point in the lives of many Eastern
Europeans.

A few days later when I saw a good friend of mine, Helen
Gaudin, I told her what I had seen in my vision and how
excited I was about the Russian people returning to harmony
with the will of God.

Five days after that, on May 17, 1967, to be exact, the first
of the wanderers I had seen making his way down the path
of defection officially came in. For on that day the State
Department announced that the chargé d'affaires of the Hungarian Embassy in Washington, D.C., had submitted his resignation to his government in Prague and had requested
political asylum in the U.S.

But this was just the beginning!

Two weeks later, on the thirty-first of May, a piece of confidential information leaked out via a newspaper. The State
Department followed it with a partial confirmation that Erne
Bernat, Press Secretary of the Hungarian Embassy and a
high-ranking officer in the Hungarian Intelligence Service,
had defected to the U.S. on April 21. His defection had been
held in the strictest confidence.

On June 28 of that same year a story in *The New York
Times* confirmed another defection from the East. The newspaper reported that Professor Ma Szu Tsung, the musician
who fled Communist China in December 1966, was lashing
out at Peking in a book in which he was accusing Peking of
a brutal campaign against the Chinese educators and intel-
lectuals.

The biggest blow to the Communist cause up to that time,
however, occurred when Colonel Yevgeny V. Runge, a
member of the Soviet State Security Committee, defected to
West Berlin on October 10. "One of the best-informed
Communist agents ever to come over to our side," a Bonn
government official proudly announced. He was also one of
the few who had successfully penetrated the security shield
of the North Atlantic Treaty Organization.

I am optimistic about the future of Russia's people. I wish, though, I would see the same bright future for Svetlana. I see her children separated from her, and I also see the distinct possibility that they will be alienated from her through Russian propaganda discrediting her. Incidentally, it has been revealed to me that one of her children will die much younger than the other one, causing great sorrow for Svetlana.

Because of my living in Washington, many of the channels of communication that are opened to me are connected with politics. During President Johnson's term in office, much of what I received had a connection one way or another with either his favorite legislative programs or with him personally. One vision that frightened my friends—even though only for a few seconds—was connected with him personally. It came to me while I was having lunch with Kay Halle, a friend of mine. Kay is the daughter and niece of the two founders of Halle's department stores of Cleveland, Ohio. She was the one who suggested to President-elect and Mrs. Kennedy that the eminent people in the arts, sciences, and humanities be invited as special guests to the Inaugural Ball so they would be recognized as the equals of the politicians —which they were and more—as the true creators of our great country.

Kay has always been fascinated with politics and her book, *Irrepressible Churchill*, written after two years of weekending at Winston Churchill's country seat in Chartwell, England, more than shows it. It was the way Churchill spoke about his being one-half American that gave Kay the idea to get a special bill through Congress, granting Winston Churchill the first honorary American citizenship ever bestowed by this nation by vote of the full Congress.

Those who have read *A Gift of Prophecy* will remember that it was she I sought when I saw the ominous black cloud lower itself over the White House. I wanted her to persuade President Kennedy not to make that fateful trip to Dallas, yet I realize now my efforts were pointless because his death was shown to me in a revelation, and a revelation of destiny can never be changed.

We had barely started our lunch in her Georgetown home when I suddenly had an uneasy feeling about President Johnson.

"Kay, listen . . ." I said hurriedly. "I'm getting something . . . I see him in the air and see some hurried decisions being made and—"

"Please stop, Jeane," Kay interrupted me with a fearful look in her eyes. "Don't tell me anything is going to happen to the Johnsons! Please! I don't want to hear it."

"It's not all as bad as that, Kay," I said reassuringly. "His life is already out of danger. There is some sort of threat—I think it is from Cuba—and because of that they are changing the President's flight plans. To make matters even more confusing for the Cubans, they are planning to land at a different airport than the one originally planned in Florida."

That same night a radio newscaster reported that, because of a rumor of a threatened Cuban "Kamikaze" attack on the presidential plane, the presidential insignia had been removed from its fuselage and, because of this threat, the flight plan of *Air Force One* had been altered.

Was there really a Cuban threat to the life of President Johnson? The White House never really admitted it, but perhaps it is better so. What I received was no doubt due to what I call "thought transference." The safety of the President at that very precarious moment was in so many people's minds that I simply *had* to receive it; the signals were that strong!

Some years ago as I was preparing to leave after having attended a luncheon given by Alabama Congressman Frank Boykin, I noticed a dark cloud engulfing Congressman Boykin when a man, two places in front of me, rested his arm on Boykin's shoulder.

When he left the congressman, the cloud went with him. . . .

When my turn came to say good-bye, I said, "Frank, I don't know who that man was who placed his arm around your shoulders, but I noticed a heavy cloud surround you while he was near you. If you have any business dealings with him at all, then you should reconsider them, for this man will get you in trouble. You will become a victim of circumstances, Frank."

"Don't you worry about it, Jeane." He smiled goodnaturedly. "Everything is made for love—just blow the cloud away."

I wish now that Frank Boykin had listened, for a short time later Frank became deeply involved in a Maryland real estate venture. Because of this and his association with his business partner, he ended up in a very precarious position. A pardon from the President was necessary to clear his name.

My favorite charity is Children to Children, Inc., and when someone offers to sponsor a charity ball and donate all of the proceeds to Children to Children, then I am thrilled to accept this honor.

Such a ball was given for me by Mrs. Ernest Medders of Muenster, Texas, in the winter of 1966.

The Medders were casual acquaintances, for I knew little about them except that they owned a beautiful farm known as Colonial Acres and were close friends of Governor Connally of Texas. Their lavish parties and their herds of red and black Angus cattle and Appaloosa horses were known for miles around.

The Medders' invitation troubled me. I wanted to attend, yet I did not want to be the bearer of ill tidings, especially to people kind enough to help my favorite charity. I had had a vision that their tremendous fortune was on the verge of disappearing, but I did not know how to break this disheartening news to them.

The date for the ball was set for a time when I had to be in Houston for a speaking engagement. Colonial Acres was situated conveniently close to the city, so afterward I rushed out to their farm, bathed, dressed, and joined the ball, escorted by Margaret and Ernest Medders.

The setting was like a fairy tale. More than a thousand guests were either dancing to the "champagne music" of Lawrence Welk's orchestra, flown in especially for the occasion, or crowding around the lavish buffet, filled with American and continental delicacies. Illuminated by the soft glow of three thousand candles, they dined and danced—and all of the proceeds of this grand soiree were to go to Children to Children.

I felt extremely grateful to the Medders for having organized such a beautiful ball.

Being an early riser, I took a refreshing morning walk before anyone else in the house began to stir. Margaret Medders joined me in my room soon after I returned to talk over all that had happened the previous night. I just *had* to tell her about my vision!

"Margaret," I interrupted her, "your money will be turned off as suddenly and abruptly as a spigot turns off a water stream."

"Money turned off?" she exclaimed, totally bewildered. "How can that be? Our attorneys have assured us time and time again that my husband's share of the inheritance will be at least five hundred million dollars!"

"How it will happen I can't say," I tried to explain gently. "All I know is that you and Ernest will not receive any more money from any inherited source. I can speak only for you and your husband. Whether your children will lose their trust funds—I don't know."

The expected fortune, as the Medders explained later to me, became tied up in legal maneuvering. They desperately fought for their inheritance, as they had not always lived the lives of millionaires, and to see "their" fortune move out of their reach was unbearable to them. They could not understand the sudden turn of events, for not only did they firmly believe that the fortune was rightfully theirs, but they had also made lavish contributions to the Democratic party and also large donations to charity. To them, it just *had* to work out . . . but it never did.

Ernest and Margaret Medders finally agreed to declare bankruptcy. He was allowed, however, to keep his 185-acre farm, inasmuch as it was protected by the Texas homesteading law.

There is a strong possibility that a motion picture company will use their story as the main theme for a new film, and if that is the case, the financial rewards will compensate greatly for their huge loss.

Often my good friends remember what I previously related to them but has been long forgotten by me. Frank Britto, for example, reminded me of a warning I made to him about his own physical condition, telling him how unwise it was to eat only one meal a day—late at night—consisting of nothing but starch, beer, and meat.

At the time I recall him grinning at me.

"That's nothing to worry about, Jeane." He laughed. "Mother Nature will take care of her own, and as yet I've had no warnings . . ."

Frank left shortly thereafter for Brazil, and my warning was forgotten until he went swimming off a lonely stretch of beach on the Brazilian shore.

"I had just gone beyond the breakers," he recalled later, "and was ready to turn around when all my strength left me. Instead, my arms and legs felt as though they were being pricked by a thousand needles. I couldn't go any farther on my own power and would have drowned had the change in the tide not carried me back to shore.

"It was then that I recalled Jeane's warning about my diet, and a thorough medical examination soon revealed that it had been the improper diet that had caused my weakened condition."

Have you ever had the experience of someone you know to be in another part of the country suddenly materializing next to you? This has happened numerous times to me but never so clearly as when Arlene Dahl appeared one day while I was taking a walk.

It had been a rough morning. I had been locked up in my office most of the time and had decided to extend my luncheon break with a short walk around the block. Suddenly I felt Arlene Dahl walking beside me.

"Today is my wedding day," she said to me. "I just wanted you to know."

She was gone as quickly as she had appeared, but I knew that this was *her* day.

I first met Arlene when she wrote me from California, informing me that she was to attend President Johnson's inaugural and would like to meet me while in Washington. I have always been very interested in her and we became friends right from the start. She is a beautiful woman with a rare eye for the better things in life, and when she appeared beside me and told me of her wedding day, I knew just what to get her—a Steuben bowl! So I bought it and mailed it off that very same day.

I later received a letter from Arlene informing me of her return from a long European honeymoon.

"We had no thought of marrying during our stay in Barbados," she wrote. "We just planned to expose our children —his two and my two—to one another and see how they would get on together. Actually, since the island then was British, we did not know a marriage would be possible."

What astonished Arlene most of all, though, was the mailing date of my present. *The postmark on the package was identical to her wedding date.* Coincidence? Both she and I sensed it was more than just that.

When Martha Rountree, of broadcasting fame, was asked to give a resumé of predictions I had made for her over the years, she reacted in her own fashion—writing them down as though she was preparing a radio or television script for a producer. In writing them down, however, she used more flattering adjectives than I would ever dare to use about myself, but for the sake of accuracy I will quote her.

"I know there are psychics," Martha wrote, "people who can close their eyes and go into a trance and, I am told, point out events yet to come. Jeane Dixon is different. She just suddenly *knows* something. It comes to her in a flash—and like a fire truck responding to an alarm, she goes into action.

"When Jeane is around you, she becomes your protector.

"From 1959 to 1963, while I was doing a news commentary on a radio network, she used to give me great leads. Following through on them, I always found a big story waiting for me.

"I often say that Jeane is 'on radar with God.' I believe this. She always seems to know when she is needed, when someone is in trouble or when danger lurks. She calls you and comes to you with her concern before you realize there is a problem.

"I wanted a house in the country more than anything else in the world. I found just the house in Virginia. Jeane pleaded with me not to purchase it, even though her husband's real estate company stood to make a good commission on it.

"She told me I would not be able to retire even though I thought I could, insisting that any house that would take me out of the public eye would be bad for me. Of course, I did not listen. When we think we know what we want, we become stubborn. I wrote out a check, handed it to her—and that was that.

"The next few months were exciting ones. At last I had my dream house. Having sold my television properties, I finally reached the point where I could look forward to that garden I wanted, watch a tree grow, write a book, or just enjoy life with my family.

"The first room completed was my daughter Martha's nursery, and I couldn't wait to move her and Miss Trolle, her nurse, into it. However, when I told Jeane that Martha and Miss Trolle would be moving, she put her foot down, irrespective of the fact that we had a caretaker and his family on the property and Lily Burns, an old friend, across the street, to keep an eye on things.

"Jeane informed me the time was not right for Martha and Miss Trolle to go—that I must take a room for them at the Mayflower Hotel where my husband and I were staying.

"Her attitude was difficult for me to comprehend. The house had been redecorated from top to bottom, and within another week or ten days my husband and I planned to make it our official residence too.

"For weeks Jeane had urged me to take out more insurance. She kept insisting that what we had was not adequate, in view of the fact that we had shipped down our entire library, all our silver, our wedding presents, my grandmother's china, my favorite furniture, rugs, and draperies.

"Since all the electrical wiring had been renewed, plus the fact that the house had been standing for over three hundred years—the original wing, that is—I thought it senseless to be overinsured.

"But if you know Jeane Dixon, you know that when she feels something, she will venture out in the dark of night, if need be, or travel from one place to another until she finds a way to prevent what she just *knows* will happen.

"So I kept Martha and Miss Trolle at the hotel, even though it seemed rather squanderous.

"Then the inevitable happened!

"My husband came down with pneumonia! Next, the worst blizzard in over one hundred years closed all roads and highways. Then, at midnight, Barney, the owner of the motel on a by-pass near our property, called to tell us that our house was all ablaze, burning beyond control! The volunteer fire-men had a rough time getting to our property—we only had well water—and to complicate matters even more, the ponds in the area were all frozen . . .

"You can guess what happened. The house burned to the ground. The fire, having started in the heating system, com-pletely spread through the interior before it was even visible from the outside. Had anyone been in the house at the time, it would have been impossible to rescue them.

"When I told Jeane about it, she commented, 'Well, I just couldn't let Martha and Miss Trolle be burned . . . She's my godchild, you know!' "

People often ask me whether I can predict the outcome of horse races. Even though I am sure God did not give me my gift for this purpose, it has nevertheless happened on several occasions that I knew the outcome of a race before it began —and often against tremendous odds.

On a rainy day in May 1967 my husband, Jimmy, and I left the office together to join Betty and Eugene Casey at the Bowie Race Track in Maryland. Eugene Casey is Chairman of the Board of Directors of the track and had invited us on numerous occasions, but somehow we had never quite found the time for it.

This time, however, after accepting his kind invitation, we found ourselves in an entirely different world. With Eugene Casey as our guide, we wandered around the clubroom of Bowie. While conversing with the assembled guests, I began to realize that this didn't just *seem* to be another world but indeed *was* another world. Conversations were spiked with race-track terminology I never knew existed. When my host explained that I was lucky because I had arrived on "getaway day"—the last day of the race when everyone tries to make "the last killing"—I laughed, for nothing was further from my mind.

What I feared soon happened. Even though I had no real

interest in the outcome of the races, all the others did. Within minutes I was pressed to pick a winner.

I glanced at Mr. Casey. He had promised that no one would ask me to forecast the outcome of the race, but by now he was powerless. Jimmy couldn't do a thing either. In fact, he did just the opposite. He gave me that certain look that means, "Please do what you can."

Pick a winner? Me? I had never asked God before for anything material. My daily prayers are always for the basic things in life: health, God's guidance in my daily activities, common sense, wisdom, and faith, but nothing material. Yet this time I felt I had to try.

Without thinking any further, I touched the amethyst-studded gold cross that I always wear, and holding it lightly, I spoke silently to God: "If I am to hear the name of a winner —I am listening . . ."

All conversation around me had ceased. Everyone seemed to be either meditating or holding their breath, waiting for me to pick a winner.

Then I heard a voice . . . a soft, soothing voice. It seemed to come from above. "Summer Sunshine," it whispered. "S-u-m-m-e-r S-u-n-s-h-i-n-e . . ."

Could I have heard it right? Was it a voice or merely my own mind asking for summer sunshine on this rainy day?

I listened again, more intently this time.

Yes, there it was again, though not as clear as the first time: "Summer Sunshine . . . Summer Sunshine . . ." And like chimes that slowly fade away on an evening's breeze, the voice became silent.

There was no doubt. This was the answer.

"Summer Sunshine," I called out loudly to the hushed crowd. "Summer Sunshine will be the winner."

The reaction was instantaneous.

"Never heard of it," one man said sneeringly. "I'm sure it's not even listed."

For a moment the group conversed excitedly while thumbing frantically through the program trying to locate the mysterious Summer Sunshine. The second race was already in progress, and if there were such a horse, it would have to be found before the next one commenced.

"Got it," someone shouted triumphantly. "She's scheduled for the sixth race." By now everyone had found it, and expectations began to mount until someone in the crowd checked the horse's previous performance.

An undercurrent of laughter broke out within a small group of men standing close at hand.

"Why, that nag has never won a race in her life," I heard one of them snicker. "This is ridiculous . . ."

I closed my eyes and smiled . . . I had accomplished what was asked of me. Their reaction was of no importance.

As the time for the sixth race rapidly approached, Betty Casey asked whether she could place a bet for me. I gave her whatever money I had with me and asked her to place it all on Summer Sunshine.

Nothing transforms a crowd of distinguished, well-dressed, well-behaved people like a horse race. All inhibitions disappear; all reserve is thrown off like a cloak. They all begin to shout the name of their favorite horse.

Betty Casey rejoined me.

"I put it all on Summer Sunshine for you, Jeane," she interrupted with a forced smile—actually feeling sorry for me.

My enthusiasm was almost drowned out by the cries that went up for Little Red Broom, the race's favorite horse, and when the horses came around the far turn and went into the home stretch, the tumult was unbearable. There was Little Red Broom leading by a length! Some of her fans in the crowd had already started counting their expected winnings, when Summer Sunshine pulled ahead, overtook Little Red Broom, and with a sudden surge of speed won the race.

The winner paid off at a rate of twenty to one.

Following my principle of never using my gift for personal profit, I took my winnings on Summer Sunshine, together with a donation from the Caseys, and used it to provide tuition, room, and board at Beckley College for a young Negro boy I was helping through school. God works in mysterious ways His wonders to perform.

A number of years ago, in 1964, to be exact, Carl van Lowe, a man who once owned a chain of supermarkets, became associated with the commercial branch of James L. Dixon and Company, Realtors. He was an able man, and when he informed us one day that he had been requested to go to Chile to establish a chain of supermarkets in that country as part of a program for underdeveloped countries, we reluctantly accepted his resignation.

As his plans progressed, I became psychically disturbed about them. I had to discipline myself continually as I listened to him explain his plans for Chile. He was full of enthusiasm. His wife, he said, would take an active part in Chilean community affairs, and he pointed out how fortunate he was to have found two able companions, Bud Greenway, a warehouse expert, and Paul Kindig, a government meat inspector, to join him in this new venture.

It took quite a while for the contract to be finalized, but once the formalities were out of the way, he began to run in a dozen directions all at once.

One morning I found him somewhat distressed. I decided to talk to him about it.

"We're going to miss you, Carl," I said to him. "We—" I suddenly stopped. Carl seemed to disappear into the wall behind him. He was more than just transparent . . . he was fading *out!*

"Carl . . ." I continued hesitantly, "I wish you would not press yourself so hard. You're making too much of this whole affair. I feel uneasy about it, for I get that you are not going to Chile at all . . ."

A smile covered his face.

"The final documents will be signed this afternoon, Jeane. You're rather late with this 'feeling.'"

In early June, Carl became seriously ill and was taken to the hospital. A week later, on June 17, the very day he and his wife were to have flown to Chile, Carl van Lowe died. . . .

In the spring of 1967, while on my way to a luncheon for Army officers' wives at Fort Myer, Virginia, I was asked who that year's Kentucky Derby winner would be.

"Proud Clarion," I answered unhesitatingly. "Proud Clarion will be the winner this year!"

When questioned afterward about how I was able to predict the winner, I had to admit that even I didn't know. I simply spoke the first name that came into my mind when I thought "Kentucky Derby."

H. L. Hunt, the well-known Texas billionaire, who had accompanied me to that luncheon, now says he wished he had taken my word for it and had put his money on Proud Clarion.

A year later, however, in 1968, he called me.

"Who will the winner be this year, Jeane?" he probed.

"Wish I could tell you," I replied thoughtfully, "but I can't. It's all so fuzzy . . . I can't get a thing. Something is wrong this year . . . there will be a mix-up of some sort."

There was a mix-up all right! Dancer's Image, the winner of the 1968 Derby, was disqualified after it had become known that he had been given a painkiller to ease the pain in his ankle.

From John Koepf, an old friend, came the prediction I once made about Vince Lombardi, the well-known coach of the Redskins football club. His recollection of the occasion is quite vivid.

"I have known Jeane Dixon for many a year," John remarked when asked about his knowledge of that specific pre-

diction. "It was in February 1968, when I was talking with her about various things, that the topic turned to football. I have been a sports fan for years, and anything that has to do with football is bound to get my full attention. Imagine my surprise when, out of a clear blue sky, Jeane suddenly interrupted the thread of our conversation and commented casually, yet pointedly, 'The Redskins are going to have a new coach!'

" 'When?' I asked, becoming very curious.

"Not this season, but soon after it."

"Boy, did I ride that one hard! 'Who is it going to be?' I queried her, determined to find out all I could about this important switch.

"She concentrated for a while, and I could see her giving it some deep thought. She frowned as though searching for more details. Then she said, 'All I see right now is an initial V . . .'

" 'The v of victory?' I teased smilingly. 'You mean the new coach is going to lead the Redskins to victory?'

" 'No, not the v of victory,' she said, slightly irritated. 'The V which I see is the initial of his first name . . . Wait!' she interrupted herself. 'I see something else . . . I see his last name beginning with an L!'

" 'Vince Lombardi!' I shouted enthusiastically. 'You mean Vince Lombardi. I can't believe it!'

"She looked up, all smiles.

" 'Yes, that is the one. I see it clearly now. Vince Lombardi will be coaching the Redskins next year!'

"While lunching with a friend at NASA a few days after Jeane's surprise prediction, I mentioned that Lombardi was going to coach the Redskins. *Did I become the laughingstock!* The guy I was with knew more about sports than I'll ever hope to know, and he just about laughed me out of the building.

"Some time later I brought it up again.

" 'I know Lombardi will coach the Redskins,' I told him

emphatically with what I thought was all the conviction needed to convince him. 'Take my word for it.'

"Laughter—even louder than before—greeted my words. 'You're at it again.' My tablemate grinned with what looked like pity. 'Why don't you give up?'

"The season came and went, and nothing happened, but I persisted in talking about Lombardi moving to the Redskins. In December 1968 my football-expert friend dropped by to see me.

" 'When are you going to forget about this ridiculous prediction of yours regarding Vince Lombardi?' he asked. 'You know Vince will never move. The odds against him moving to the Washington Redskins are about one in a million. If, however, it should happen, then count on a great lunch in a restaurant of your choice. O.K.?'

"A few weeks later I received a card from him with a simple one-line message.

" 'Vince moved to Washington. Where do you want to eat?'

"I called him on the phone, the smell of victory still in my nostrils.

" 'Forget about the lunch,' I said in closing after we had discussed Vince Lombardi's move to the Redskins. 'I knew he was going to move here all along. Jeane Dixon told me!'

" 'If I had only known that, I wouldn't have thought of contradicting you,' were his sourly spoken parting remarks."

As I was lunching one day with Lorene and James Melton, Lorene asked her husband to show me the pictures of his new boat. He just "happened" to have a picture of it in his wallet, and he was all smiles as he handed the colored photograph to me across the table.

It showed a handsome craft with James standing on the flying bridge.

As I looked at the picture of the boat, I saw its lines becoming dimmer and dimmer while another boat appeared in its stead.

"Jimmy," I soft-toned his enthusiasm, "you will not keep this boat very long. I see a—"

"Stop it, Jeane!" he interrupted. "I won't let you take that beautiful boat away from me!"

But I continued on. In glowing terms I described his new boat to him, but he just would not listen.

A scant two months later when he bought his new boat, he felt slightly embarrassed for not having listened to me.

When a psychic vision is not fulfilled as expected, it is not because what has been shown me is not correct; it is because I have not interpreted the symbols correctly. When this occurs, it fills me with regret and a fervent desire to ask for more guidance the next time I have to interpret a vision or dream that seems too symbolic to be easily understood right from the start.

I wish now I had interpreted the symbols correctly when I experienced a dream that dealt with the future of members of my immediate family.

It started with a call from my sister-in-law, Mildred Pinckert. She phoned me from California last year to inform me that my brother, Erny, was to undergo surgery the next day.

"Please, Jeane," she pleaded, "pray for Erny, and see if you can find out whether the operation will be successful!"

I prayed that night for an answer and fell asleep with my mind focused on Erny's future.

It was early the next morning, shortly before dawn, when the answer came to me in a semi-dream.

I saw Erny and Mildred walking together. She looked extremely beautiful in a lovely bright-red dress with a high neck, flowing long sleeves, and a skirt that touched the floor. What impressed me most, though, was a candle she was holding in front of her. It was a short burned-down piece of candle that I knew had once been long—very long. The golden flame flickered as she moved and went out altogether as she stood in front of Erny. . . .

I called Mildred as soon as I awakened.

"Don't worry about Erny," I said. "He will be all right. He will be with you all the days of your life."

Erny's operation was a complete success, but *Mildred* died a short time later. *I should have known this—for it was all in my semi-dream.* If I had not been so completely caught up in Erny's welfare, I would not have stopped after conveying to her that Erny would recover. I would have advised her to see a doctor herself lest her life be snuffed out like a candle before Erny's.

Sometimes I have visions that are unexplainable due to the fact that the information I receive is incomplete. Such was the case when several members of our office staff and I attended the wedding of Iletha Herring, another member of our staff, two summers ago. It was while sitting with the congregation, watching the bride and groom standing before the altar, that I saw Death enter the quiet church.

Weddings are such lovely ceremonies that I just did not expect this to happen; but he was there—uninvited and mournful in every way. He was represented by two ominous-looking coffins draped in black which I saw resting behind Iletha and her groom—patiently waiting to be filled.

I naturally felt sad when I should have been happy. Could the coffins be there for Iletha and her new husband? The vision didn't say. I wasn't shown who was to die, or why. Seeing the two coffins, however, made me realize that two of the people involved in this wedding would soon be called to judgment.

On the way home I told members of my staff about the vision. I requested them to regard it as confidential, inasmuch as I did not want anyone in Iletha's close circle of friends to be alarmed.

A few weeks after Iletha's wedding the expected happened. Word reached us that the best man in the wedding had drowned. His sudden passing was followed two weeks later by the accidental death of the groom's brother. Both of them were in the wedding party.

The future holds in store for us both life and death. Pat Parker Headley will gladly testify to this!

After losing her husband in the manner I predicted she would (see *A Gift of Prophecy*), we became very close and saw a great deal of one another.

Many times she came over to our house to use the piano to finish composing a concerto she was dedicating to her brother. Pat, though a charming person, in my opinion did not have the perseverance necessary to be a vocational composer.

I am an incurable matchmaker, and when I saw Pat getting interested in Dr. Lee Williams, a most successful nose, ear, and throat specialist, I waited patiently on the sidelines, using immeasurable quantities of self-discipline. I *knew* what was going to take place, and I was so eager to tell her about it.

Then came the night of the concert. In every way this was Pat's night. The evening centered around her as soloist with the National Air Force Symphony Orchestra playing the concerto she had written for her brother. With Dr. Williams sitting beside me, I saw Pat playing with all her heart. Suddenly he reacted.

"I love her," I heard him thinking. "I love her."

I was delighted, for this I knew was part of her future.

Being good friends, Pat and I were quite frank with each other. After the wedding we had a quiet heart-to-heart talk, and I told her that the wedding was only the beginning of happiness for her.

"You are going to have a baby, Pat," I told her with a heart full of happiness. "I know that during your twelve years of marriage to your first husband you had been told by your doctor that you would never have any children. He was wrong. I can see you rocking an adorable little boy in your arms."

Several months later she became pregnant and I very much wanted to join her in her happiness, but I couldn't.

"I just can't be happy about this pregnancy," I told my secretary. "This is not the baby I saw in her arms . . ."

Pat lost the baby, and after consoling her, I pointed out to her that she would still get the little boy I predicted.

"I knew you would end up losing this baby," I said, "but the happiness your little son will give you will more than make up for it . . . and I want to be his godmother!"

Today Philip Lee Williams is a growing boy and has more than replaced the sadness that accompanied the earlier years.

Quite often predictions and good friends seem to go hand in hand, perhaps because I think of them so often. Take my friendship with Louise and Harold Mott, for example. We have known each other since the day I made a prediction about her baby in 1945. A mutual friend of ours sent Louise to me when she appeared to be extremely upset over the health of her child.

"Can you tell me what's wrong with my baby?" she asked pleadingly. "Does he have anything that can be cured? He seems all right when he is lying in my arms, but somehow he becomes ill when I hold him up. What can I do?"

One look convinced me that her child was at a low ebb. I was shown psychically that he would not live very much longer and that the surgery to be performed on him would be unsuccessful.

I told the truth I had seen.

When her husband returned from his overseas duty, they checked immediately with a specialist surgeon who recommended surgery. He felt the problem was caused by a slight pressure on the brain and could possibly be resolved through an operation.

Surgery was performed but to no avail. The little boy died.

After the funeral Louise came to see me.

"No more children for me, Jeane," she declared emphatically. "All my love is for my little girl from now on."

"I see it differently, Louise," I said happily. "I see you with not just one but three little girls!"

She laughed.

"Where from?" she countered. "I have no plans for any more."

Three months later she called.

"I am pregnant, Jeane," she announced breathlessly. "Your prediction seems to be coming true." The story repeated itself when she found she was pregnant *again* a year and a half after the birth of her second girl.

"You are responsible for the last two," she remarked on the day she called to tell me the good news. Of course, I was not responsible for either—I was only a messenger.

One evening while Jimmy and I were having dinner with some friends in late 1966, I felt a sudden urge to get to a telephone and call Louise.

"Your second daughter has just had a minor automobile accident, but it is nothing to worry about," I assured her. "You might, however, suggest to her to stay out of cars for the next few weeks."

After her daughter returned home that evening, Louise told her of my warning.

"We just had the accident Mrs. Dixon predicted," her daughter said surprisedly. "It was nothing but a little dent and a scraped fender . . ."

One thing my warning did, though, was to make her especially careful. She deliberately avoided cars but almost slipped one night, as Louise told me later, when a very special boyfriend asked her to go to a party with him.

"She was on the verge of going but decided against it at the last moment," confessed Louise. "Good thing she did.

The boy got involved in an almost fatal accident en route to the party and will be hospitalized for weeks. If she had accompanied him, she might not be alive today."

I made a third prediction for Louise about three years ago just as I was preparing to fly to California. In my haste I was not able to reach her, so I phoned her sister Rachel in New York.

"Tell Louise to be easy with Harold when he tells her that he is giving up his law offices and is going to free-lance. What he is planning to do is really for the best and everything will work out just fine."

When Rachel relayed my message to her sister, the reaction was almost equally predictable.

"Can you imagine my hearing this from *Jeane* first and not from my own husband?" she said with a dazed look in her eyes. "I eat, sleep, and drink with the guy, but he never told me that *this* was what he was working on!"

I was not clairvoyant in this case; it was merely thought transference that made me aware of Harold's plans.

My last prediction dealing with Louise and Harold occurred in the spring of 1967 when Louise phoned and told me excitedly that she was going to redecorate her entire house.

"You ought to see me now," she said, catching her breath in between words. "I am holding the phone in one hand and a batch of fabric swatches in the other, and I am drowning in wallpaper books, paint charts, and fabric samples."

"Hold on, Louise," I said. "Slow down. While you were talking I saw men carrying furniture out of your house. It is pretty clear to me that you will be moving soon."

"That can't be right, Jeane," she reacted. "We have no moving plans whatsoever!"

"Wait anyway," I suggested, "for I do see you moving. I do not know where, but I see you leaving this house."

On my advice she postponed all decorating plans and did not pick up her wallpaper books, paint charts, and fabric samples again *until after she had moved into a new home in Arizona.*

Harold, it appeared, had once again, through thought transference, told me of his plans. . . .

There are some who have the occasional gift for physical and mental healing. There have been a few occasions in my life which suggest that I, too, have been used as a channel for God's healing power.

An interesting example of this is the experience I had with James J. Harkins, Service Director for the Newbury Guild, a firm which produces deluxe greeting cards.

In September 1966, when I first met Mr. Harkins during one of his business trips to the nation's capital, I noticed that his right hand was completely covered with warts, one of them seemingly inflamed and—as he afterward indicated—quite painful. Neither one of us mentioned the warts during our first meeting; however, I was concerned about them.

Later on that same day a very surprised James, while washing his hands, discovered that all his warts had disappeared. That moment could have been a coincidence.

Since that time, whenever Jim Harkins is in town, we meet at St. Matthew's Cathedral at seven in the morning to take our early morning devotions. You get to know much about a person's life this way, and soon he was confiding in me.

For twelve long years—as I presently learned—he had been plagued with unceasing pain in his legs and thighs. Sometimes it became so bad he stuffed pillows under his legs when traveling by train, and if he had to motor any distance at all, he would have his feet and ankles strapped for support.

On June 28, 1967, at ten minutes to three in the morning, he awoke feeling a strange sensation similar to a mild electric shock travel through his entire body, down his legs, and then fade away.

Early the next morning he phoned me and was very excited.

"Did I ever tell you that this pain of mine has been getting worse lately?"

"No," I replied, "but I knew it anyway. You stumbled rather clumsily one morning as we left St. Matthew's because —and this I felt—you were experiencing such pain . . ."

"You really felt the pain?" he asked, surprised.

"Yes, and I have prayed for you ever since."

It was then he told me what had happened. When he described how the shock had affected him and later disappeared, I knew right then that God had healed him. This time it could not have been a coincidence.

As of this writing more than a year has passed, and Jim Harkins is still pain-free.

In 1966 Lady Bumgardner, Louise and Harold Mott, and I flew to Fort Smith, Arkansas, where I was driven from one bookstore to another in order to autograph copies of *A Gift of Prophecy* as they were being sold. Midway in our itinerary Louise asked our driver to make a short detour to enable us to stop at Porter's Restaurant.

"B. A. Porter, the owner, is a good friend of mine," Louise explained as we rode along. "He has been ill for months, and all the doctors inform him that it seems to be caused by a deeply ingrained virus. Nothing they prescribe for him helps. He drags himself to the restaurant, stays for a few hours, and then goes home, returning to bed again. I just wanted to stop by and say 'Hello.'"

Mr. Porter, looking very ill indeed, was waiting for us.

As our brief visit drew to a close, I took his hand and said, sensing how devout a man he was, "God bless you. I will pray for you."

Together we said our first prayer for the return of his health. I prayed sincerely and asked God to heal him if it were His will.

I have since heard from Mr. Porter.

His pains left him the moment he walked back to the

restaurant kitchen after my departure. His lost strength also returned as if by a miracle. Now, I am told, he prays for *me* every day.

One of the most touching examples of healing came about, not instantaneously, but as a result of my being able to diagnose a problem which doctors could not see. It is the story of Mary Alice Riesenman. When I first became acquainted with this case, she was two and a half years old and had not yet walked a step in her life. Her father, Dr. F. Regis Riesenman, the well-known psychic researcher and psychiatrist, had, in the course of attempting to discover a cure for her, consulted the finest orthopedic and pediatric specialists. In addition, he had taken his little daughter to the International Institute for Mental Health where she was kept under close observation for five frightening weeks.

The experts all agreed. Mary Alice, they claimed, had cerebral palsy brought on either by an injury at time of birth or resulting from a serious illness which occurred when she was only one month old.

Being familiar with the psychic ability of Peter Hurkos, Dr. Riesenman, in desperation, sent a few articles of Mary Alice's clothing to him. Mr. Hurkos, who has been able to divine hitherto unknown facts concerning people through physical contact with some of their possessions, replied that Mary Alice would walk on her third birthday, December 21, 1960, and that on Christmas day of that year would make her way to the tree to pick up her presents.

It happened as Peter Hurkos predicted.

This was sufficient encouragement for Dr. Riesenman to continue, and she was fitted with orthopedic shoes and was given corrective exercises to develop her leg muscles, despite his firm belief that Mary Alice would never become fully agile because of the cerebral palsy.

On an occasion four years later Dr. Riesenman proudly

showed me a family photograph of himself, his wife, and their five children.

"Is this Mary Alice?" I asked, pointing to one of the little girls in the picture.

He nodded.

"Then let me tell you what is wrong with her," I said, and I crossed my office in an exaggerated duck walk. "This is how she walks"—I showed him—"and this is the way she walks up the stairs." And throwing my right leg up and out, I proceeded to climb the stairs.

Surprise and interest showed in his eyes.

"Exactly," he said. "You're right . . . but you have never seen her walk. How do you know this?"

"Do you know why she does this?" I asked politely, postponing an answer to his question.

"Oh yes," he replied, and began to give me her medical history to the minutest detail.

"Let me tell you what is wrong," I interrupted. "Mary Alice does *not* have cerebral palsy. She was born with a congenital dislocation of her hips. At this time nature is forming new sockets, and she will continue to improve and will begin to walk better. She will not need surgery."

It was a thankful Dr. Riesenman who reported my findings to a famous orthopedic specialist. X-rays confirmed what I had told him. A new series of exercises were prescribed for Mary Alice, and it was agreed that, inasmuch as nature had taken over, the planned surgery would not be necessary.

These are some of the perceptions and experiences I have had during a lifetime of trying to bring my life into harmony with God's will by fulfilling His purpose for me on this earth and by using the gifts He has given me to the best of my ability.

There are two other psychic visions I have had which greatly affected Americans, and they are important enough to be given separate consideration in the following chapters: the assassination of Martin Luther King, Jr., and the assassination of Senator Robert F. Kennedy—both of which have reshaped the course of history.

6

Death of a Dreamer

"I have a dream today . . .

"I have a dream that my four little children will one day live in a nation where they will not be judged by the color of their skin, but by the content of their character . . .

"When we let freedom ring, when we let it ring from every village and every hamlet, from every state and every city, we will be able to speed up that day when all of God's children, black and white, Jews and Gentiles, Protestants and Catholics, will be able to join hands and sing in the words of that old Negro spiritual:

" 'Free at last! Free at last! Thank God Almighty, we are free at last . . .' "

(Martin Luther King, Jr., Summer, 1963)

"And then I got into Memphis. And some began to say the threats—or talk about the threats that were out. Or what would happen to me from some of our sick white brothers.

"Well, I don't know what will happen now. We've got some difficult days ahead. But it really doesn't matter with me now. Because I've been to the mountain top. I won't mind.

"Like anybody, I would like to live a long life. Longevity has its place. But I'm not concerned about that now. I just want to do God's will.

"And He's allowed me to go up to the mountain. And I've looked over, and I've seen the Promised Land.

"So I'm happy tonight. I'm not worried about anything. I'm not fearing any man . . . 'Mine eyes have seen the glory of the coming of the Lord.'"

(Martin Luther King, Jr., April 3, 1968)

"And when they saw him afar off, even before he came near unto them, they conspired against him to slay him.

"And they said one to another, Behold, this dreamer cometh.

"Come now therefore, and let us slay him, and cast him into some pit, and we will say, Some evil beast hath devoured him: and we shall see what will become of his dreams . . ."

(Genesis 37:18–20)

And on April 4, 1968, a dreamer was slain. . . .

A conspiracy? An act of hatred by one single individual? Officially we may never know, but I knew that Martin Luther King, Jr., would eventually be assassinated as far back as 1960.

"His usefulness will be over in 1968," I told my husband Jimmy and some of our close friends at a gathering at that time. "I feel strongly that, in order to obtain the rapid advancement Dr. King desires for his people, he will begin to use known Communists, with the belief that he will be better able to serve his people. Instead of his being used, however, the Communists will turn the tables on him and will start using the Negro movement to serve their own aims. Once they have infiltrated the Negro movement, Dr. King will no longer be of use to the Communist cause—and they will eliminate him.

"This," I went on to predict, "will happen in 1968 when his usefulness to them will be ended. He will suffer a violent death."

When I say Martin Luther King and the Communists worked together, I do not imply that he was a Communist or that he backed the Communist conspiracy as such within the United States. I do feel, however, that their influence on him was sufficient to say that he had become an unwitting tool of the Communists.

This information came to me *not* in a revelation but through telepathy. I had indications as early as 1948 that Communists within the United States were planning their infiltration of the Negro movement, but it was not until 1960 that they began to plan the assassination of the man who would be leading the Negroes in their civil rights struggle in 1968.

For years the movement grew, and on January 29, 1964, FBI Director J. Edgar Hoover testified before a House subcommittee:

"[The Communist party] strives only to exploit what are often legitimate Negro complaints and grievances for the advancement of Communist objectives.

"Controversial or potentially controversial racial issues are deliberately and avidly seized upon by Communists for the fullest possible exploitation.

"Racial incidents are magnified and dramatized by Communists in an effort to generate racial tensions. *As a result, such campaigns are actually utilized as a stepping stone to extend Communist influence among the Negroes.*"

There is no doubt that Mr. Hoover had facts to back him up. In fact, the *Congressional Record* of July 29, 1963, contains information from the files of the House Committee on Un-American Activities relating to *fifty-nine* of the officers, members of the board of directors, legal, health, and other committees of the NAACP. These records indicate that between them these members have been associated with more than 450 organizations identified as Communist fronts by the U.S. Government. While many members have only a limited number of past or present affiliations with these organizations, some have impressively more. A founder and key official of the NAACP, for example, the late W. E. B. DuBois, had no less than ninety-six Communist-front affiliations.

I felt this connection long before official inquiries came up with the hard facts.

In 1955 a man described by Dr. King as a "brilliant, efficient and dedicated organizer and one of the best and most persuasive interpreters of nonviolence," Mr. Bayard Rustin, joined Dr. King as a close and trusted adviser. However, in the past Mr. Rustin had been a member of the Young Communist League group at City College in New York. Even though he claimed to have resigned from the YCL in the early 40s, he still worked closely with organizations such as the War Resisters League, which I deem questionable. His activities also included working in and with the American Forum for Socialist Education, which has been cited by the Senate Internal Security Subcommittee as a Communist front.

In 1957 Mr. Rustin attended the sixteenth national convention of the Communist party of the United States and later in 1958, according to the *Congressional Record* of August 13, 1963, the same Mr. Rustin made a trip to Russia to participate in a meeting of the Nonviolent Action Committee Against Nuclear Weapons.

Today, however, the same Mr. Bayard Rustin is the Executive Director of the A. Philip Randolph Institute and also Chairman of the Executive Committee of the Leadership Conference on Civil Rights.

There is no doubt that while Dr. King sought to formally organize the Negro movement, "other" elements were present right from the beginning, for when he formed the Southern Christian Leadership Conference in March of 1957, Dr. Fred Shuttlesworth was there with him.

Who is Dr. Shuttlesworth?

Dr. Shuttlesworth during the 1960's was the president of the Southern Conference Educational Fund, and that is where the difficulty lies. According to a Report of the hearings of the Senate Internal Security Subcommittee held March, 1954, "The Southern Conference Educational Fund, Inc., was initially an adjunct of the Southern Conference for Human Welfare. After the exposure of the Southern Conference for Human Welfare as a Communist front, it began to wither and was finally dissolved, but the Southern Conference Educational Fund, Inc., continued. The official paper, the Southern Patriot, which was published by the Southern Conference for Human Welfare, was taken over by the Southern Conference Educational Fund, Inc., which professes the same ostensible purpose."

"The Southern Conference for Human Welfare was conceived, financed, and set up by the Communist Party in 1938 as a mass organization to promote communism throughout the Southern States. Earl Browder, former general secretary of the Communist Party in the United States, in a public hearing, identified the Southern Conference for Human Welfare as one of the Communist Party's 'transmission belts.' Under date of March 29, 1944, the Southern Conference for Human Welfare was cited by the Special Committee on Un-American Activities as a Communist front . . .'"

In 1960, when Bayard Rustin moved out of Dr. King's close circle of advisers, another man, Jack H. O'Dell, also known as Hunter Pitts O'Dell, took his place.

Who is O'Dell?

A two-volume study entitled *Structure and Organization of the Communist Party of the United States*, published by the House Committee on Un-American Activities, has a list on page 576 of those elected to the national committee of the Communist party of the U.S.A. as known to the Committee in November 1961.

Hunter Pitts O'Dell is listed there. . . .

Another name of interest in connection with this story of

infiltration is that of Dr. James A. Dombrowski. He, incidentally, was one of the people who moved from the Southern Conference for Human Welfare to the Southern Conference Educational Fund.

It was Dr. James A. Dombrowski who was identified at the Senate Internal Security Subcommittee hearings in March of 1954 as a member of the Communist party by another admitted Communist, John Butler, a former official of the party's Alabama chapter.

Dr. King was aware of this.

"King has cooperated closely with the Southern Conference Educational Fund since our last report," according to Committee counsel Jack Rogers of the Louisiana Joint Legislative Committee on Un-American Activities in a Committee publication dealing with the activities of the Southern Conference Educational Fund, Inc., in Louisiana. "He [King] filed a lengthy affidavit in the Federal Court in New Orleans strongly supporting James A. Dombrowski and the Southern Conference Educational Fund as 'integrationists' of good character. When I saw this affidavit, I sent King three copies of our first report on the Southern Conference Educational Fund by air-mail, special delivery; and I sent him word through his attorney, Wiley A. Branton, Atlanta, Georgia, that he, King, could appear in Court in New Orleans and repudiate the affidavit if he so desired, on the basis of having been given evidence of the Communist connections and leadership of the Southern Conference Educational Fund . . . If King were ever inclined to cleanse himself of the taint of Communism, this would have been a very excellent opportunity, well justified under the circumstances. I regret to inform the Committee that no answer, whatsoever, was received from Martin Luther King, and his affidavit still stands in the court record in New Orleans, in spite of his certain knowledge of the true character of the Communist leadership of the Southern Conference Educational Fund."

Dr. Martin Luther King, Jr.'s circle of advisers had been infiltrated with Communists and he apparently did not object because he wanted to use their money, their contacts, and their organizational genius for the advancement of his own people.

"I am sick and tired of people saying this movement has been infiltrated by Communists and Communist sympathizers," he was quoted as saying in the New York *World-Telegram,* July 23, 1964. "There are as many Communists in this freedom movement as there are Eskimos in Florida."

Robert F. Kennedy, then attorney general, agreed with him for reasons unknown to us.

"Based on all available information from the FBI and other sources," he commented, "we have no evidence that any of the top leaders of the major civil rights groups are Communists or Communist controlled. This is true as to Dr. Martin Luther King, Jr., about whom particular accusations were made, as well as other leaders."

Yet what I have quoted here is only but a small portion of the available evidence stacked high in the Library of Congress, pointing toward heavy infiltration by the Communists within the civil rights movement.

During the last year before Dr. King's death, my conviction that the year 1968 was to be his final year gained strength and came into sharp focus.

On the Monday of that fateful week in April my husband asked me to deliver some confidential papers to the late Frank W. Boykin, former congressman from Alabama and later chairman of the board of the Tensaw Land and Timber Company.

The Boykins have been friends of ours for many years, and seeing Frank and his wife has always been a pleasure.

"Stay and have lunch with us, Jeane," Mrs. Boykin coaxed. "It's such a nice day . . ."

So I joined them and their other guests for lunch on the
roof of the Washington Hotel. . . .

✛✛✛✛

"I remember that day very well," Frank Boykin recalled.
*"We were having lunch in the dining room on the roof of
the hotel. Next to us sat Mayor Washington, discussing politics with a couple of newspaper people . . . his table was
just about touching ours . . .*

*"My mind went back to the happy years I had spent in
Washington as an Alabama congressman, and my love for the
city and our way of life was so great that I just couldn't agree
with the idea of thousands of people using it for another
protest march . . .*

*" 'I've been talking to a lot of people down South lately,'
I said to Jeane, 'and they're all worried about this trouble and
everything, and I hate to see Martin Luther King get here
and organize another march on the city.*

*" 'I have a meeting planned with Congressman Charles
Halleck, Connie Rivers, Bob Sikes, and Armstead Seldon in
the hope of getting an injunction to keep King and his thousands of followers from marching on Washington . . . because
wherever he goes, trouble follows sooner or later . . .'*

"Jeane looked up from her plate and touched my hand.

*" 'Don't you worry about that, Frank,' she said somewhat
sadly. 'Martin Luther King will not get to Washington . . .
he will be shot before he can get here. He will be shot in
the neck . . .'*

*" 'But he's planning to come here within the next few days
to organize this thing,' I said, startled and unbelieving. 'Don't
tell me he'll get shot that soon . . .'*

*" 'Just that soon,' she emphasized. 'He will never get here.
He will be shot first . . . and Robert Kennedy will be
next!' "*

✛✛✛✛

I left the hotel and returned to my office.

A man had called while I was out and insisted on speaking with me. Finally, convinced that I was not available, he had asked my receptionist, Barbara, to take a message and he firmly instructed her to be certain that I received it.

"Tell Mrs. Dixon that before the end of the week the flag on the White House will be flying at half-staff . . . She will understand."

That was his message.

On Wednesday of that same week another call came. This time the call was referred to Victor Rand.

"Be sure that Mrs. Dixon gets my message. Tell her that there is no doubt—the White House flag will be at half-staff before this week is out."

Mr. Rand told me about it when I returned to my office later that day.

He seemed upset and worried, although he had no knowledge of the previous call taken by Barbara.

He explained, somewhat nervously, that he was impressed by the cultured voice of the caller but confused by his insistent manner and the obscurity of his message. Mr. Rand said he pressed the caller for an explanation, but the caller only answered:

"Just tell Mrs. Dixon what I told you . . . she'll understand."

Mr. Rand concluded: "And with that he hung up. What did he mean, Mrs. Dixon?"

"He means that Martin Luther King, Jr., will be assassinated before the end of the week!"

In the evening of that fateful day Mrs. Nancy Smith and I were dining at Blackie's House of Beef. While we were enjoying the visit of the owners, Mr. and Mrs. Ulysses Auger, at our table, a man who had been watching the teletype machine which is set up in the corridor of the restaurant tore off a length of tape from the machine, walked a few steps to our table, and calmly handed the strip of tape to me, as he said:

"Here, Mrs. Dixon, is your forecast. Martin Luther King is dead."

With the Communists, assassination is never the job of one man. Conspiracy is part of the communistic ideology, and Martin Luther King, Jr., was the victim of just such a conspiracy.

I have received psychically that the man who killed Dr. King is not James Earl Ray (who is not a Communist). He was involved in the plot, but he did not know the extent of the conspiracy until he was too deeply involved to be able to pull out. He does not know the true names of the others involved in the assassination plot, but he can recognize his "contact" if he is brought face to face with him. He only knows the man under his assumed name . . . I was able to tune in on his "contact's" channel and have seen the name change.

I see four people planning the final steps of the assassination. I see them plot the last-minute details with precision.

First there is a young man, medium height, blond, in his early thirties. I see him gesturing, discussing, thinking . . . Then there is the man who did the actual killing. He is in his late twenties or early thirties. He is white, of medium build, and soft-spoken. He is a Communist or an experienced assassin used by the Communists. He was involved in the plot right from the beginning, when it was planned at an entirely different place than Memphis. Again, I must emphasize this: the assassination was not a spontaneous act. It was premeditated. Some of the close associates of Dr. Martin Luther King, Jr., were in on it, and these are the people who arranged the final details that led to his assassination.

The assassins have not completely succeeded in making Ray the scapegoat for the entire affair. In a copyrighted article *U.S. News and World Report,* March 24, 1969, listed a number of unanswered questions.

"Adding fuel to widespread suspicion of conspiracy," the magazine reports, "were these developments:

* "Ray told the court at his 2½ hour proceeding that he disagreed with various 'theories' that there was no conspiracy to kill Dr. King. But he did not elaborate on his statement.

* "In Washington, the Justice Department disclosed that the 'investigation into the original allegations of a conspiracy is still open.'

* "Dr. King's widow, Coretta, and many other Negroes doubted Ray had acted alone. Said Mrs. King, 'This plea of guilty cannot be allowed to close the case, to end the search for the many fingers which helped pull the trigger.'

* "John Larry Ray, a brother of the convicted man, told the St. Louis *Post-Dispatch:* 'My brother said there was someone else in on this deal, but it has been hushed up by the Federal Bureau of Investigation.'

* "The Senate Internal Security Subcommittee announced it was assembling evidence bearing on a possible conspiracy. Said the chairman, Senator James O. Eastland (Dem.), of Mississippi:

"'There are some things about this affair that indicate to me there may have been a conspiracy.' . . ."

"Ray's record also was cited to indicate his past ineptness at crime.

"Yet, it was pointed out, he managed to carry out the assassination of a national figure in almost perfect fashion, and then to elude one of the world's most extensive manhunts for two months while he crossed international borders without hindrance."

There are other questions that need answering if opponents of the belief that there was indeed a conspiracy involved want to silence all opposition.

There was nothing in Ray's background to indicate fanaticism. He had no apparent reason for wanting to kill Martin Luther King.

Why then, if Ray was cool and organized enough to bring off the killing by renting a flophouse room, locking himself in the bathroom and killing King with just one shot, did he panic and leave his rifle behind—the only thing that could tie him to the murder?

There is nothing in his background that suggests the necessary contacts or organizational planning essential to arrange his false identities and his elaborate escape to Europe. This took more than usual planning and more money than Ray ever before possessed.

Where did he get the estimated $10,000 he spent during the time he escaped from the Missouri State Penitentiary in April 1967 until he was captured in London on June 8?

With the death of Martin Luther King, that leaves one more person who might become potentially dangerous to the Communists—his wife, Coretta King.

"Mrs. King has much the same charisma as her husband," *Newsweek*, March 24, 1969, reports. "Everywhere she goes, a mob of ardent admirers, black and white alike, seems to materialize almost at once . . . At first Coretta carried her message with Martin's words. Shortly after the assassination she appeared in his stead at an antiwar rally in New York and for her text used notes he had left behind. But as she continued to fulfill his long list of appearances, she has developed her own ideology. This is rooted in what she understands to be King's developing philosophy . . . She scorns U.S. involvement in Vietnam's 'civil war' and asks 'amnesty' for draft resisters and Army deserters."

"Reverend Abernathy fell heir to Dr. King's position," explains one Northern civil rights leader. "But the keeper of the image is Mrs. King."

It is here that I see future problems.

Coretta King will become very active in politics, where her personal magnetism and fearlessness will serve her well.

Her determination, however, will lead her into serious trouble with other members of the Negro community. I see the same people who were exerting their Communist doctrines on Dr. King now trying to use his wife as they had used him. Because of circumstances her own people will turn against her eventually, and in the years to come she will be in great danger of losing her life.

Her activities will not be understood and will tear the Negro movement into several factions instead of unifying it.

Martin Luther King, Jr., dedicated the last years of his life to the cause of social and economic justice for his people and for all people. In his well-motivated but misguided obsession he believed he could bring about the good he sought by manipulating Communist infiltrators and resources to serve his purpose. Because of this serious miscalculation his life was taken and his movement suffered a deep division. His cause was great; his means were not.

But the impact of his life and work will continue to be felt in the years ahead.

7

The Death of Robert, The Son of Job

When RFK died, it was not because he had to die. His life could have been longer and more productive—yet he chose to die. Some called it "the will of God."

It was not that way at all. I know, because all of the visions I received about the pending death of Senator Robert F. Kennedy were reflections of thoughts of men. Men planned his death, not God. I simply tuned in on their channels and their plans were exposed to me.

I "saw" him die—

Yet I know he could have lengthened his life if he had only listened . . .

In a previous chapter I pointed out that the vibrations of the members of the Kennedy family are extremely powerful and that much of what they plan or what happens to them is continuously revealed to me.

In the Biblical book of Job, Chapter 1, Job lost all his sons because Satan willed it and God allowed it to happen.

This story has a tragic sequel.

It came to me in a dream when I saw the Biblical patriarch Job appear out of the distant past and walk up to a lonely Joseph Kennedy, embracing him with a tender, understanding touch. I turned toward Job and looked into his face. It was furrowed by sorrow and compassion, and streaks of dried-up tears showed on his sun-scorched face.

I looked at Joe . . . and saw his face distorted by anguish and grief. An uncontrollable fear showed in his eyes when he turned his head and recognized the face of Job . . .

"What do you want?" I could feel his mind plead. "Why do you embrace me? What do *we* have in common?" And fright dimmed the majestic glow of his aura while he seemed to wait for the answer . . .

But Joseph Kennedy knew the answer, and so did I! I have always known that tragedy would stalk the Kennedy family. I saw it happen to John Kennedy, and I knew that Robert would follow.

When on April 4, 1968, I told Frank and Ocllo Boykin that Martin Luther King, Jr., would be shot, followed by Robert F. Kennedy, it was not the first time I had shared my vision regarding RFK's death. But finally on September 13, 1967, I felt that it was imperative to inform Senator Robert Kennedy personally about this danger to his life and selected James Fahey, author of *Pacific War Diary* and a close friend of both the Kennedys and myself, to be my ambassador in trying to bring us together.

⊁⊱⊹⊰⊁

"*On September 13, 1967, I made one of my occasional visits to the capital,*" *Jim Fahey recalled when asked about that first attempt at establishing direct communication between Jeane Dixon and Robert Kennedy, "and stopped by to see Jeane.*

"*'You have got to do something for me, Jim,' she said with a note of urgency in her voice. 'I've got to see Senator Robert Kennedy—it is extremely important. I have an autographed copy of my book,* A Gift of Prophecy, *for the senator, and when you give it to him, please tell him that I must see him on a matter of grave importance . . . I hope he understands.'*

"*My reception was as usual when I arrived at Bobby's office.*

" 'Good to see you, Jim.' He smiled. 'Is there anything special I can do for you today?'

"This was my chance! I grabbed it!

" 'Yes, Bobby, there is. Jeane Dixon has asked me to present you this autographed copy of her book, and she said she wants to see you. She asked me to tell you this!'

"I know, to say it 'hit him like a bomb' is so stereotyped, but nevertheless that was the way he reacted to it. He reeled back and then stopped. Slowly his head went down until his eyes gazed at the floor in front of him. I realized my message had hit him hard . . . and for a brief moment I thought he was going to reply, but nothing came of it . . . silence was the only tangible reaction.

"Several moments passed before I broke the deathly stillness of the room.

" 'I have to go now, Bobby. I have an appointment to see Senator Ralph Yarborough of Texas.'

"Senator Kennedy looked up wearily but otherwise unmoved.

" 'Give him my regards, Jim,' he said softly. 'Thanks for stopping by . . .'

"I wondered whether he really meant it this time.

"After returning to Jeane's office, I told her of Robert Kennedy's reaction. She looked disappointed but didn't comment.

"Later on that same year I wrote him a letter, again stating that I thought he should get in touch with Jeane Dixon. I suggested that it might be done informally.

"Bobby never replied."

✠✠✠✠

After addressing a convention of stockholders and franchise holders of the Kentucky Fried Chicken organization during January 1968 in Miami Beach, Florida, I asked the audience whether they had any specific questions, which is my custom after giving a speech.

At the particular time, many of the questions dealt with the same subject.

"Will Robert Kennedy ever become President of the United States?" asked one of the stockholders. My answer was direct and unconditional. "No," I replied. "He will never become President of the United States."

I remember this question so clearly, because it surprised me that no one pressed for more details. To the audience, it was just one of many questions, and once the answer had been given, they passed over it and proceeded to the next one. Also, at that time Senator Kennedy had not as yet announced his candidacy for the Presidency, thus it seemed only a matter of relatively minor importance.

Being businessmen, they eventually turned the discussion to their own company.

"Is it advisable to buy more stock in Kentucky Fried Chicken?" inquired a member of the audience.

"It most certainly is," I answered, "for I see that it will split very, very soon!" (Since that time it has already split twice.)

That same evening approximately fourteen conventioneers joined me in my suite at the Hotel Fontainebleau. With them was my friend Jim Matthews, President of the Topps Drive-In restaurant chain in the Washington, D.C., area—now Vice-President and member of the board of Gino's, Inc., an organization controlling 170 restaurants. But it was Frank Callahan, a public relations executive with a Philadelphia firm, who wanted to know more about my Kennedy prediction.

"Are you certain that Robert Kennedy will never reach the Presidency?" he said.

"Yes, Mr. Callahan," I answered. "I get it that he will be assassinated in California this coming June." At that time I did not predict that it would be in Los Angeles, but I knew it would be in California.

It was a thoughtful group of people that left my suite that night.

"*After Jeane spoke before the banquet of our Kentucky Fried Chicken Convention,*" Jim Matthews recalled, "*a few of us went up to her suite in the hotel. With me was Frank Callahan, an executive with the advertising agency of Lewis and Gilman in Philadelphia which handles our account. Frank was very anxious to meet Jeane, so he came along.*

"*There must have been slightly more than ten people there that night, and somebody joked, 'Okay, Jeane, give us some more predictions.'*

"'*I will,*' she answered, '*but keep this one quiet for the time being. I will give you more details on my prediction concerning Senator Kennedy. He will never become President because he will be assassinated in California this June. He will meet a fate similar to that of his brother Jack.*'

"*Also in the same breath, she told us that we would get into serious trouble with North Korea . . . and strangely enough the North Koreans captured the USS Pueblo a few days later.*

"*Anyway, a few days after the assassination of the senator we had a commercial recording scheduled here in Washington for Colonel Sanders. Frank Callahan came down from Philadelphia and with him came Gus Cacoran and our account executive.*

"*Frank entered the studio and walked straight up to me with a rather strange look in his eyes.*

"*Jim, I want to tell you something. When I returned to Philadelphia after Jeane made that prediction to us about Robert Kennedy in her hotel suite, I told Gus about it. He wouldn't believe me. "Frankly," he said, "I can't believe that anyone could have the power to foresee events like that so far into the future."*

"'*He has since changed his mind.*'

"'*Sure have,*' Gus broke in. '*I'll tell you from now on I will believe anything she predicts. I'm convinced!*'"

✠✠✠✠

The threat of the assassination of Robert Kennedy remained with me, and on March 29, 1968, while speaking at the Theta Sigma Phi celebrity breakfast in Fort Worth, Texas, I again predicted his death to Mia Whitehead, who accompanied me, to members of the greeting committee, and to the wife of Senator John Tower of Texas.

"He will be shot," I remarked impulsively, "while in California!"

On March 4, 1968, James Fahey had another meeting with Senator Kennedy and left his office convinced that the senator somehow sensed that eternity had begun to close in on him.

"I was in Washington in connection with Jeane Dixon's Children to Children Foundation," related Fahey, "and I dropped by her office. Jeane was detained, so I walked upstairs to see her husband. While waiting I picked up a newspaper, and the first thing that caught my eye was a column by Bob Duke, one of the staff writers of the Mobile, Alabama, Register. It was datelined Tuesday morning, February 20, 1968.

"JEANE DIXON PREDICTS SELDEN IN, BOBBY OUT," the headline said. 'Washington seeress Jeane Dixon told a captivated crowd of more than 5,000 persons here Monday night that U.S. Senator Robert F. Kennedy will never be elected President.' It went on to list more predictions dealing with U.S. politics, but they didn't interest me. Why would she say that he would never become President? He wasn't even in the running!

"When I saw Jeane later that day, I didn't mention the newspaper story, nor did I mention it to Bobby when I saw him the next morning. I was certain that by this time he would not be intimidated by whatever Jeane Dixon might predict for him. But on this specific occasion I recognized the first sign that even though Bobby might not run from a pre-

dicted death or defeat, he sensed that something was imminent. It became obvious when I gave him a little St. Patrick's plaque that I had picked up in Boston.

"It was a small, simple thing, with St. Patrick on one side and a three-line poem on the other.

"Bobby read it:

" 'May You Be in Heaven Half an Hour Before the Devil Knows You're Dead,' it said.

"His hand trembled as his eyes followed the words, but the smile I expected never materialized.

"He didn't speak . . . in fact, his reaction to it was very similar to the one I got when I told him that Jeane Dixon wanted to see him. He just stared at it. His eyes were sad and melancholy when he finally looked up at me.

"A week following that meeting I saw him again, but this time he was on television announcing his decision to run for the Presidency. The whole thing then fell into place: Jeane Dixon's urgent request to see him, his reaction to my poem, the sad expression in his eyes . . . I ran scared, and looked for ways to reach him and tell him he would never make it. . . .

"The chance came when, on May 27, 1968, I visited Dave Powers in his office at the Federal Records Center in Waltham, Massachusetts. Dave was formerly one of President Kennedy's White House aides and our friendship dates back to the time when I presented a copy of my book, Pacific War Diary, to the President.

"I dropped in now to renew our acquaintance and at the same time to ask him to press Bobby for a conference with Jeane.

" 'Dave,' I said soberly, 'I've got news that will knock you over. It deals with Robert Kennedy and Jeane Dixon. I know that you intend to go to Ireland this week with Joan and Eunice Kennedy for the dedication of the President Kennedy Park. Will you tell Joan that I think she should organize a

*small family meeting and invite Jeane because she must speak
to Robert?'*

" *'Want to tell me about it?' he asked.*

" *'Can't, Dave . . . wish I could.'*

" *'Okay, I'll tell her . . .'*

*"The next time I saw Dave was on July 5, a month after
the assassination. . . ."*

✠✠✠✠

Our friend, the late Congressman Frank Boykin of Alabama, also attempted to warn the Kennedys of the futility of
Robert Kennedy's endeavor to run for the Presidency, but
again to no avail.

*"When Jeane predicted the death of Martin Luther King
and that of Robert Kennedy in the same breath during our
luncheon at the Washington Hotel, it came as no surprise to
me," commented the congressman.*

*"She was always talking about Bobby never making it . . .
but King and Kennedy—and seemingly within such a short
time of each other—both of them were causing so much
trouble . . . Bobby was always advising what all of the Negroes should do, and he didn't understand . . . he never
earned a nickel in his life, nor did he ever have to work. . . .*

"I tried to warn him, but he wouldn't listen.

*"His dad, Joe Kennedy, is one of the finest friends I have.
In the good ole days he used to head the U.S. Maritime
Commission while I was the vice-chairman of the Merchant
Marine Committee. We've been friends for over thirty-five
years and are very close.*

*"One time, while some of us were lunching at his place in
Hyannisport, Joe stood up and paid me the nicest compli-
ment any man could ever give to any one.*

*" 'If I had only one more friend like Frank Boykin,' he
told the group, 'I wouldn't need any more friends.' I guess it
was because of our close relationship that he contacted me*

*later on to ask me if I would do something with Bobby . . .
but nobody could, you know.*

*"Jeane Dixon told me repeatedly that something would
happen to Bobby. He wouldn't listen to anyone. He went
his own way.*

*"Some time ago Joe called me on the phone just as I was
giving a banquet for 165 senators and congressmen and said:*

*" 'Frank, try to get hold of Bobby and see what you can do
with him.'*

*" 'Joe,' I said, 'you know I can't do anything with him. He
won't listen. He just wants to do everything . . . everything
in the world, you know . . .'*

*" 'I know,' he said desperately. 'Then see if you can get
Howard Smith to talk to him.'*

*"So I phoned Congressman Smith, and he and Bobby talked
at length.*

*"You know Bobby was just rampant," Frank Boykin con-
cluded. "Jack was so different. He was a kindhearted man."*

✠✠✠

Even though I experienced many premonitions regarding
RFK's death, I was convinced that he really did not have to
die as I had predicted. Yet the feeling that it would nevertheless happen became stronger and stronger until that final day,
May 28, 1968, when I realized with certainty that death was
finally and irrevocably closing in on him.

I was addressing a convention in the Grand Ballroom of
the Ambassador Hotel in Los Angeles that day, and when,
at the close of my speech, I invited questions from the floor,
the question that seemed to be in everyone's mind was the
first to be asked.

"Will Bobby become President of the United States?" a
lady asked, and a tense, expectant audience waited for the
answer.

The answer came to me with a fierce, unrelenting finality.
It came in the form of a black curtain that descended

between the audience and me when Robert Kennedy's name was mentioned. It dropped down like lightning and did not stop until it had reached the floor. It was black . . . it was swift . . . and it was final!

I saw it clearly.

"No, he will not. He will never be President of the United States," I answered calmly, "because of a tragedy right here in this hotel."

I repeated this after the meeting to Captain George Maines, an American Legion official, and to Mrs. June Wright, mother-in-law of the lieutenant governor of Florida, who were with me.

"Do you think we should inform the hotel management?" I asked.

"Please, Jeane, don't!" Captain Maines replied, visibly shaken. "Bobby Kennedy is due to speak here next week, and it would only worry them."

June Wright did not agree with him. She decided to make a serious effort to reach her friend Rose Kennedy, the senator's mother, who was staying at the Ambassador Hotel that night. June confessed to me later that she placed three calls to Mrs. Rose Kennedy, leaving messages, asking her to return the calls in order to inform her of the prediction, but Mrs. Kennedy ignored the calls. June Wright never got the chance to warn her.

As we made our way out of the ballroom via the kitchen corridor, I suddenly sensed Death . . . He was all over, filling the entire corridor with everything that was dark and evil. Utter blackness surrounded me and threatening currents closed in on me from all sides. I recoiled and must have looked stricken, for George Maines cried out:

"What's wrong, Jeane? What is happening?"

His voice brought me back to reality.

"Robert Kennedy . . . This is the place where he will be shot, George! I see him falling to the floor covered with blood . . ."

*I am sure it was the day the killer had completed his plans
in his mind and selected the spot for assassination.*

"*My determination to eliminate R.F.K. is becoming more
the more of an unshakable obsession please pay to the
Order . . . R.F.K. must die,*" *he wrote in his diary on May
18, 1968.*

"*Robert F. Kennedy must be assassinated before 5 June
68 . . . I have never heard please pay to the order of of of
of of of of of of this or that.*

"*R.F.K. must be disposed of like his brother was.*"

As Sirhan Bishara Sirhan wrote these words, he was filled
with an insane hatred and drenched with a compulsion to kill.

And while I was in Washington developing plans to increase the effectiveness of Children to Children, Inc., and
Robert Kennedy was preaching his doctrine of new politics
and the need for a continuation of his brother's policies, the
Arab assassin-to-be wended his way to the Lock, Stock 'n
Barrel Gun Shop in Pasadena, California, and asked for low-
powered bullets "to use on the target range." The shop was
sold out. "Then give me your best," said Sirhan, and he purchased two boxes of much more powerful dum-dum-like Mini-
Mags.

For the next few days he could be found twice a day
practicing rapid firing with his .22-caliber pistol.

And on June 5, in the early morning hours, one of Sirhan
Bishara Sirhan's Mini-Mags finally hit its predestined mark
and extinguished the spark of life that had made RFK a man.

The murder trial of Sirhan Bishara Sirhan turned out to be
a great disappointment for the young assassin—strange as that
may seem.

He has become a great hero in the eyes of the Arab world
and, deep inside, would like to receive not only the death
penalty but also undergo the actual execution. He is convinced that his act was an act of pure patriotism and his death

would make him a martyr. He wants to be the one for whom
they will erect a statue and go down on the pages of history
as *the* one who helped the Arabian cause.

✠✠✠✠

"*The next time I saw Dave Powers,*" said Fahey, "*was one
month after the assassination.*

"'*Did you give Joan Kennedy the message about Jeane
wanting to see Bobby?*' *I asked.*

"*His eyes reflected a sadness and an inner emotional
struggle for self-control as he answered:*

"'*No, it slipped my mind. There was so much to do during
that trip . . . your message just slipped my mind,*' *and he
shook his head as if to erase an unpleasant memory. 'Are you
free to tell me now what it was all about?*'

"'*Jeane Dixon predicted that Bobby would never become
President of the United States. She also predicted his death,*'
I countered sadly.

"*Remorse deepened by sadness showed on his face, as he
realized the true meaning of the forgotten message.*

"*Could he have possibly prevented the death of RFK? I
want to believe he could have, for Jeane always said that
Robert Kennedy's death did not have to take place.*

"*Maybe that's what went through the mind of Dave Powers.
Could his relaying of the message have altered the course of
history, or is it possible that if the message had been delivered
to Mrs. Rose Kennedy, RFK still would not have wanted to
listen?*

"*Only God knows.*"

The personal magnetism and driving energy of Robert
Kennedy attracted the hopes and aspirations of millions of
Americans—particularly young Americans.

His sudden and violent death was a deep shock to all
Americans and will be recalled in the years ahead as one of
the major signs of the turbulent times in which he lived.

8

On the Threshold of the Future

Visions, telepathic messages, psychic feelings—they all give me a deep knowledge of what is to take place in our generation and beyond, and when I announce these often cataclysmic events, I experience great anxiety. I know that many of these events would not transpire if humanity would just listen to the voice of God.

Sometimes visions and telepathic messages come in such rapid succession that it seems as though they are struggling for priority; I feel this constantly, and the more visions I experience, the deeper my compassion becomes for troubled humanity. Mankind will never be able to create a world of peace without faith in and love for the King of Peace. As a mere channel of communication, all I can do is point to the dangers ahead and hope and pray that those who can hear will heed.

It is in this function of "messenger" that I relate the following predictions as they were revealed to me.

RUSSIA MAJOR INTERNATIONAL PROBLEM

Repeatedly over the past few years I have warned that Russia has no desire to abolish her aim for world domination. While I have seen the U.S.S.R. shipping war supplies to Vietnam, Korea, Algeria, Central America, and Cuba, and using Cuba as a jumping-off base for infiltration of the Latin

American countries, I also observed the Russians hiding numerous inter-continental ballistic missiles under Cuban elementary schools to forestall any attempt on our part to destroy them. A surprising development of the past year is the ever-increasing presence of Russian submarines operating near the Bolivian coastline. Why their weapons are aimed toward Bolivia I do not know. It may be, however, part of the overall Russian design to bring the entire world under its domination.

As early as 1948 this "grand design" for world domination began to take shape in my mind through telepathy, and it has evolved through the years into the following pattern:

SOVIET COMMUNIST STRATEGY
(Non-nuclear)

AIM: To increase the number of Soviet-controlled dictatorships by the destruction of capitalism, domination of the Socialist world, subversion and economic penetration of non-Soviet-bloc areas, and neutralization—if possible through treaties—of the use of atomic and thermonuclear weapons.

TIME SCHEDULE:

1955–1960
1. Disrupt NATO, SEATO, and Bagdad pacts.
2. Avoid war with the West at all cost.
3. Gain maximum penetration of the Middle East and Southeast Asia, short of a direct war with the U.S.
4. Increase political pressure in Africa, north of the Equator.

1960–1975
1. No war in Europe; no war with the U.S.
2. Keep up the pressure in Southeast Asia and keep the U.S. involved.

3. Secure the Middle East from the Nile to the Khyber Pass; deny U.S. access to Middle East oil.
4. Secure all areas from Yugoslavia to Kenya, including the Mediterranean.
5. Secure the Philippines and Indonesia.

1975–1980
1. Europe, India, and Japan join the Soviet-bloc economy.
2. Leave Australia, Rhodesia, and South Africa to the U.S.
3. Use bold initiative and work for domination of Latin America.
4. Create chaotic conditions for U.S. economy.

1980–1990
1. Consolidate Soviet-bloc holdings in the Eastern Hemisphere.
2. Increase economic and subversive pressures in Western Hemisphere; war with the U.S. if necessary.

1990–2000
1. Absorb the Western Hemisphere by all means necessary including an atomic war if needed.

While this is the Russian master plan as I perceive it, it is not at all certain that they will succeed in their grand conquest. But one cannot deny that their influence is spreading with rapidity and that their subversive activities are felt not only in countries such as those in the Middle East but in student uprisings in America and in Europe. These student uprisings will continue to spread throughout the world.

I have seen two Arabs acting as Soviet intermediaries. One

looks like a typical Arab—dark hair, dark eyes, and a goatee. I do not know his complete name, but I have seen parts of his name. The second man appears older, has white hair, a rather round face, and wears a white turban. I recall that his name was rather long and began with the letter S.

These two men have been active in paying off the Arabs for their guerrilla attacks on Israel. This is done with gold coins that have the appearance of U.S. coins yet are minted with Siberian gold in the U.S.S.R. They are coins of one, five, ten, and twenty dollars. I saw the gold leaving Siberia and watched the coins being minted. Later on I saw evidence of these coins being closely examined in Washington and observed our authorities establish their Russian origin. *The total amount minted in the last twenty years is in the hundreds of millions of dollars.* This minting process, incidentally, still continues.

Acting as advisers and organizers of student uprisings and protest strikes is another specialty of the Russian organizational geniuses. For a considerable length of time now I have warned that race riots and student unrests have been, and still are, instigated, financed, and controlled by Communists. In the fall of 1968 I saw a man whose name appeared in a psychic vision only with the letters *D-E-M-I* . . . traveling from city to city, meeting with disillusioned racial elements and potential student leaders, organizing riots and demonstrations. "Demi . . ."—now known to me from newspaper reports as Pyotr N. Demichev—is a valued member of the Russian KGB (Bureau of State Security) and works in this specific function directly under Mikhail A. Suslov. His vibrations are strictly "Moscow." Lately, however, I have observed him traveling in Europe and Africa. A few months ago he journeyed to France after having spent some time organizing uprisings in England. *He is the man behind many of the race riots that have plagued numerous nations.*

The timing of many racial and student riots is determined, unbelievable as this may seem, by the three men who control the Central Committee of the U.S.S.R.; Mikhail A. Suslov is at present in overall charge. Boris M. Ponamarev is the man in control of foreign Communist parties, while Yuri V. Andropov seems to be in complete charge of all affairs dealing with Communist parties in the satellite countries. Together these men control Aleksei Kosygin, Leonid Brezhnev, and the military establishment of the Soviet Union.

I have also seen that the Russians are interested in Vietnam at the present time only as an effective means of diverting American attention from Europe. Their chief aim is still West Germany and Berlin in particular. Several times during 1968 I warned some of our leading senators about the danger our country will be facing if we should ratify the much-publicized Nuclear Non-proliferation Treaty. Russia wants this treaty to go into effect as soon as possible but will not sign until the German Federal Republic has been pressured into signing. Only then will the U.S.S.R. commit itself. They are convinced their unconventional military power is greater than that of the Western world, and once the treaty has gone into effect, they will seriously consider marching into Western Germany inasmuch as the treaty will not allow us to use nuclear weapons to stop their overpowering hordes. *I predict that if and when they execute this plan, we will not go to war over it.* Some people may argue that NATO will not tolerate this; in answer to that, let me say this: *the signing of the Nuclear Non-proliferation Treaty marks the beginning of the end of NATO.* This organization will become rather ineffective, starting in 1970, for prior to the end of that year most interested nations will have ratified the treaty, and the Russian inspectors will be allowed to check NATO activities.

LAND-BASED MISSILE THREAT INCREASING

In the summer of 1967, while speaking to the wives of our high-ranking military personnel and their guests at Fort Myer,

Virginia, I reported that I had seen a long mountain range in which were stored hundreds of missiles, many of them trained on the free Western European nations.

At the start of my talk I did not know the name of these mountains, but then suddenly it flashed before my eyes— "Carpathian Mountains" was the name—and I did not hesitate one moment to use it in my speech. It came to me, I am certain, through telepathy, from one or more of the representatives of the Iron Curtain countries who had been invited to this meeting.

At my mention of the Carpathians the wife of an official of a supposedly neutral nation leaped to her feet and stated that she would not remain to hear her country publicly accused. Since I had mentioned no country in particular—and my world atlas showed that the Carpathians are part of several Eastern European nations—her action seemed to be most injudicious but revealing.

Since that time I have concentrated more deeply on the matter of the Carpathian missile threat, and the total number of missiles trained on Western Europe from those mountains now number 750!

KOREA AND VIETNAM

The same Russians who dictated the conduct of the Korean war, Suslov, Ponamarev, and Andropov, are also setting policy in the Vietnamese war. For years now, in the face of optimistic announcements by our high officials, I have seen the ghastly specter of death and destruction in Vietnam. In every speech I have made during the past few years I have stated that this war would continue, despite the auspicious reports to the nations by politicians and generals. I saw, and still see, more American blood being shed on the battlefields. I have always tied the future of Vietnam and Korea together, for politically they are one and the same problem. They figure in the Russian plan to keep the United States occupied in the East while the Russians set their goals for conquests in the West. I see death and destruction continuing to rage in both Vietnam and Korea. The peace negotiations of 1969 regarding the future of Vietnam will produce a temporary peace—but the fighting will flare up again. As long as the Russians have not executed their plans for Western Germany, they will keep us involved in Vietnam. They will also try to ensnare us in Peru and other Latin American countries. Their main goal, however, at this time, is to keep us away from Germany.

DISARMAMENT A FARCE

The discussions for world disarmament will continue for some years to come, but while some nations are actually going to disarm as a result of the negotiations, the leaders of the countries that are holding the talks have absolutely no intention to disarm. These leaders will work and talk total disarmament, and they will agree—as Russia will agree—to international inspection, but they do this because by that time they will have secret testing facilities perfected to the extent that they will be safe from inspection.

There will be a great peace movement then and even more so after the conclusion of the disarmament talks. The false security that will accompany this movement will lull the majority of our people and many of our political leaders to sleep. The money saved as a result of the disarmament will be turned into the expansion of the consumer industry, but it will lead to great destruction, for while peace seems to be on everyone's mind, sudden destruction and war will occur in 1999.

In the 2030's a man who will have gained a reputation as a "peacemaker," great in informational stature, and much admired, will emerge as the "war lord" of modern times. The entire nation will back him, believing that he who has been so strong in peace can also be victorious in war. He will have military power at his disposal and will possess greater might than anyone ever before him and will use it to combat the Red Chinese menace that will by that time be fighting in Russia and the Scandinavian countries. His changeover from peacemaker to military genius and dictator will be so sudden and abrupt and so absolute that people for the first time in modern history will wake up and realize that they have been had! For this will be why he entered politics!

THE END OF CASTRO IS IN SIGHT

Cuba's dictator, Fidel Castro, is rapidly losing both influence and power in his island government. On each occasion that I concentrate on him I see that his days in power are numbered because he is no longer useful to his Communist bosses. The Cuban government is not only dominated by the Russians, but Suslov himself is dictating Cuban affairs directly from Moscow. Cuba has become a problem of the first magnitude to the Soviets. If it had not been for the fact that Raoul Castro, now a Communist political commissar, has been protecting his brother, Fidel might already have been removed. I sense that he feels sudden death lurking around the corner and that it will not be a natural one. Raoul's influence, too, is declining. Every time I meditate on him I see a large ball rolling away, getting smaller and smaller as it rolls . . . which indicates to me that he will eventually also lose his power and usefulness to Moscow. Fidel's death, however, will not mark the end of Communism in Cuba. The country has become a training base for North Korean, Thai, Burmese, Algerian, and African guerrillas. These men are trained by Chinese instructors, working under Russian command. South American guerrillas and others intended to operate in the Western world—including scores of U.S. militant Negroes— are trained by the Russians themselves. The future of Cuba will become a major source of contention between China and the U.S.S.R.

FOOD SHORTAGE DUE TO EDUCATIONAL NEGLECT

We are in extreme danger of directing our educational efforts too much toward the highly technical fields and not placing enough emphasis on subjects dealing with agriculture. We are in dire need of a balance in education. I predict a serious food shortage creeping up after 1979 if no steps are taken to eradicate the imbalance in our educational system. All our resources, all of our advanced technical knowledge are being geared toward conquest of outer space, but we neglect the good earth that makes all this possible.

COMET WILL HIT OUR EARTH

I have seen a comet strike our earth around the middle of the 1980's. Earthquakes and tidal waves will befall us as a result of the tremendous impact of this heavenly body in one of our great oceans. It may well become known as one of the worst disasters of the twentieth century. Although the approximate location of the point of impact has been made known to me, I do not feel I should reveal it at this time, but I will provide a more detailed warning at a future date.

THE POPULATION PROBLEM

Recently Mr. Robert McNamara went on record as stating that a world-wide family-planning effort, "on humane but massive scale," is necessary to avoid "catastrophic consequences." Speaking at Notre Dame University, he continued his warning by saying that "if there is anything certain about the population explosion, it is that, if it is not dealt with reasonably, it will in fact explode in suffering, explode in violence, explode in inhumanity."

Mr. McNamara is wrong. I do not foresee anything of this sort. True, we have a population problem, but this is nothing new. Every society and generation has had its problems, *but there will be no catastrophic consequences.* We will not have to rely on "the pill" or other contraceptive methods. Rather, improved education and family guidance will become the accepted solution and will make people aware of their responsibilities as both parents and citizens.

SPLIT IN THE CATHOLIC CHURCH

Within the next twenty years the Catholic Church will undergo more drastic changes in doctrine and tradition than ever before in history. Steadily increasing numbers of priests and high-ranking officials will apply for permission to marry—and will end up marrying with or without permission. The Church will become so divided in matters of dogma and principle that it will split into many factions. There will, however, be many who will hold fast to the old ways and will not cast loose the traditions of the Church. They have always lived by it, prayed by it, and will die for it.

THE U.S. SUPREME COURT

In a public speech I made during the period in 1968 when the name of Justice Abe Fortas had been placed in nomination for Chief Justice of the Supreme Court, a member of the audience asked, "Will Abe Fortas become Chief Justice?" I answered that I did not see him as Chief Justice, and in fact I did not see him remaining for long on the Court.

I now predict that President Nixon will appoint five new Supreme Court justices during his term in office.

PRESIDENT NIXON

Contrary to what is being rumored, President Nixon is not being misled by those on his staff who persist in telling him that the present Soviet leadership is weak, divided, and confused. He is fully aware of the real facts! Tuning in on Russia, I get harmonious vibrations emanating from the very core of the Soviet hierarchy, showing strong, united, and politically active leadership with gradually progressing plans to divide *our* leadership and peoples.

President Nixon will come up with a surprising solution to a very important matter, and I see that it is advisable for the President to rely on his *own* judgment in this matter. The President does have foresight and he should use and trust it. I get that the President need not seek moral support to forge ahead in his own decision . . . this is important. The people —not only in America, but internationally—will not understand why this important and far-reaching decision was made thus and so, but the future will prove his decision to be a wise one. His progress will be slow but sure.

I see where the President will be firm and resolute in his decisions in the following matters:

1. Foreign affairs and their effect on domestic affairs.
2. East-West trade.
3. Student disorders.

Under the first heading comes the Vietnamese war, which is very, very important; the second could seriously affect our country's economy adversely, and the third is tied in directly with subversive plans for world revolution.

I sense that if the President is not firm, the world will be in serious trouble. President Nixon is our last hope. As I have said repeatedly, I see building up in our country "a government within a government" which may be successful in stopping the President's major decisions and causing not only the United States, but the entire world, untold trouble!

I see danger now—unless our President properly guides the United States foreign policy, we can expect turmoil and rebellion in the midst of affluence. This situation could only lead more and more to repressive measures—which, in the end, could seriously affect our precious and singular freedom.

Wherever I speak, the question is asked over and over— what about Vietnam? At the moment this is the most important matter of foreign policy and is uppermost in the minds of every American.

I see that hastening the training and equipping of the South Vietnamese forces and supplying them with enough conventional arms will solve our problem in large degree—for then I see that we can begin to withdraw our soldiers and let the South Vietnamese fight and win their war against the Communists. But the President is being advised, and foolishly, against taking such a course.

LAIRD AND "CREDIBILITY GAP"

I get telepathically that Secretary of Defense Melvin Laird wants to keep the public advised as much as possible—to erase the so-called "credibility gap" born during the last administration. Of course this does not mean that he will give out information that should be kept secret for the sake of national security.

The Secretary will soon advise the public that our reconnaissance plane was shot down by North Korea because the plane was interfering somehow with secret Russian underwater electronic weapons. I feel that the shot which actually downed the plane came from the ocean's surface—probably from a ship—and that there was at least one survivor. In the instant that I "saw" the explosion I also saw a number on a gun—it looked like the figure 37.

OLD CRISIS

The price of gold will rise, our dollar position will become precarious, and the government will have problems in preventing financial panic.

ANTI-RIOT MEASURES

Our President and the governors of the fifty states will announce a new approach and a new firmness in dealing with some of the professors who incite and join in agitating the students.

EAST-WEST TRADE

On this subject it seems as though my vibrations are all going one way, and I see that right now we do not have a balance of trade between the East and West, which is regrettable as this has always been the most economically healthy status for our world.

I see that our supplies of strategic materials are being diverted and are falling into the hands of the Communists so they may carry on their plan for world revolution and domination. This is a very serious situation, as there must be balanced two-way traffic carrying goods for peace, not war, if the world is to survive the Communist plans for takeover.

We are dealing, I feel, with a Communist-bloc cartel that covers the entire world—and unless this situation is understood and resolved, it could destroy many countries through complete disruption of the economic structures. I feel strongly that in this area the Soviet Merchant Marine is very influential. I see many ships flying the Hammer and Sickle . . . but few flying the Stars and Stripes. However, I do feel our Secretary of Defense will strongly advise the present administration—and the public—that the need for building more ships should be given a "number one" priority, and now! Otherwise, as I have predicted for many years, the year 1970 will find the U.S.S.R. as the undisputed power of the seas as well as the skyways.

SPECIAL RIOT FUND

I see a greater influx of foreign money coming into America than ever before. This "special fund" money is being used to finance student riots on the campuses of our country as well as the race riots.

The militant leaders are directed by the U.S.S.R., which is now stepping up the momentum. They will push heavily for more and more agitation, rioting, and violence, all timed accordingly with their master plan to "divide and conquer!"

KENNEDY'S 1972 PRESIDENTIAL BID

I feel the Kennedy machinations stronger than ever. Senator Edward Kennedy will endeavor to capture the 1972 Democratic presidential nomination; however, there are potent, dangerous vibrations around him which could alter the course of his life. Senator Kennedy, in attempting to run for President in 1972, is reaching ahead of his natural timing, and while charisma and financial power—both of which he has in full measure—are very important, still there is for each of us on this earth a timing—originated and guided by a power greater than all telling—and going against this timing is not wise.

I see the good senator a bit premature in his bid for the Presidency in 1972.

CHANGES IN GREAT BRITAIN

England will probably have a general election in the near future, as there will be changes in the top echelon of the government—changes which can result only from a general election. Too, I get that a person of prominence in England will pass from the picture and will be nationally mourned.

Great Britain will be called upon this year to broaden her military activities because of an international crisis, which will also cause much confusion and talk in our own country. This crisis and resulting confusion will cause indecision on a matter of grave international proportions and will be recorded in the annals of history.

England is clearly headed for trouble with her present government, and I see many, many changes.

FRANCE'S SITUATION WORSENING

I get that it was not at all wise to vote General de Gaulle out. France is now in a very precarious condition—both internally and externally. Soon there will be great violence and even much talk of assassination of French leaders.

France, regrettably, is not going to be better off for the recent change in government. This will prove a grave mistake. I guess you might say for France that hindsight will prove better than foresight. There will be a complete reorganization of the government, but the French will come very close to revolution, if not actually have one.

As I see it, France should watch closely the foreigner who came to Paris in 1967 to organize the paralyzing labor strikes that have virtually brought France's economy to a point of regression.

BERNADETTE DEVLIN

Bernadette Devlin, elected to the English Parliament from Belfast, and the youngest woman ever to be seated in the House of Commons, will become a great orator. I foresee a brilliant future for her. True greatness lies ahead of her. I see only one possible stumbling block—timing. Her higher aspirations must be kept under control, and she must try not to forge ahead too quickly. She is young—only twenty-one —and has many years ahead of her.

She will come out with all kinds of new ideas and at times will be a bit rebellious against conservative submission to convention.

As a student of history and political science, she will reel off situations regarding history and will make history herself.

As time goes by, Miss Devlin will have great influence over others—not only her people, but also her political colleagues, and not only orally, but also through her writing.

She will have more than one marriage in her life, but success in her work will always be first and foremost.

Because she is so sure of her convictions, she will have great opposition at times—and this could cause deep, bitter, and lasting enemies.

PEACE IN IRELAND

The political-religious trouble in Ireland will seethe for a while longer, then end. The end to this trouble will come *as soon as the influence of certain American, self-righteous groups is eliminated;* however, I do not get the timing on this.

UNEXPLAINED SUBMARINE LOSSES

For a long time now, in fact ever since the fall of 1968, I have been waiting for the British to announce the loss of one of their submarines. I experienced the vision concerning this tragedy in early January 1969, and even though they never acknowledged this loss, I know it happened. They will, however, reveal at an opportune time that one of their submarines never returned.

Submarine losses have been in the news ever since the Russians placed their highly sophisticated and deadly accurate underwater missiles in strategic points in the Atlantic, the Pacific, and the Mediterranean waters. In 1965 I warned of this development. I publicly conveyed this warning to the U.S. Navy, telling them that they were quickly falling behind the U.S.S.R. in the development of underwater missiles. Using the oceans as testing areas, the Russians have successfully destroyed one Israeli, one French, two U.S., and one British submarine. In the case of the last United States loss, the USS *Scorpion,* I knew that it would meet with complete disaster a half year before it actually happened, yet at that time the name was still obscure to me. The actual name *Scorpion* came through as early as three months preceding the tragedy. Again I warned of it in numerous speeches, and again it was politely ignored.

In the case of the *Scorpion,* I saw a missile rise up from the ocean floor and follow the *Scorpion* in what appeared to be a "tunnel" of swirling water surrounded by billions of tiny sparks or air bubbles. The missile tracked the submarine in its own wake until it was close enough to exert its immobilizing force. The next thing I realized was that all electrical circuits of the doomed ship had ceased to function, and I saw it sink down onto the ocean floor—ever so gently. I do not know whether the missile actually destroyed the ship after it had touched bottom, or whether it was the tremendous water pressure that closed in for the final kill. Prior to this attack, the USS *Thresher* and its crew met a similar fate.

This "MIRV of the sea" is a man-made monster. When I saw its destructive power in action, I warned the U.S. Navy of this development. To confuse our desperate search for the missing sub, Soviet submarines broadcast misleading signals which were picked up by our ships, drawing them away from the disaster area.

I pleaded with our officials to inform the American people about these treacherous activities of the Soviet nuclear submarines, but no one ever did.

JAPAN—A NEW POWER

For some time now I have seen Japan preparing itself for a gigantic economic power struggle with the West. It will move ahead to become one of the world's greatest economic powers, and this, in turn, will not only produce political problems in the Far East as well as in the Western world, but will also create serious internal problems within the United States as it will affect the structure and influence of the labor unions and movement.

THE MIDDLE EAST CONTROVERSY

Even though the United Nations and the big powers will press for a solution to the Middle East problem between the Arabs and the Israelis, I see nothing but continuing trouble in that part of the world. Peace between the belligerents is still a long way off. Their disagreement will only cease to exist after the great earthquake that will hit Jerusalem.

Until that time, however, there will be no real solution for the Arab-Israeli problem. Constant tension, hot diplomatic debates, border clashes and heavy fighting, interrupted by occasional respites of forced cease-fires, will characterize life in the Middle East. I have projected my quest for information into the year 2000 and see Chinese and Mongol troops invading the Middle East. I see devastating battles raging uncontrollably east of the Jordan River. It is a war of East against West. It will be an almost futile fight against an overwhelming foe—but the Lord will place Himself at the side of Israel, and great losses will be suffered by the Orientals.

After the tide of battle has shifted, Israel will become one of the greatest miracles of all times, for the Israelites will then realize that it was God's intervention that brought about this ultimate victory, and they will finally accept Jesus Christ as the Son of God.

MILITANTS UNDER FOREIGN CONTROL

I see racial turbulence continuing for some time in this country and spreading throughout the world. The militants and those Negroes abetted by the murder of Martin Luther King, Jr., will create more strife and more turmoil. I do not as yet see them replaced by leaders loyal to *our* country. Only when truly loyal leaders take over the militant movements do I see racial tension leave the scene. I see little hope for this, however, as long as many militants take direct orders from the U.S.S.R.

GERM WARFARE

In a recent vision I have seen that one of our most influential national institutions is being used as a cover-up for chemical and bacteriological warfare experiments. As this sort of activity is completely alien to the normal work of this organization, no one will ever suspect it. I do get, however, that their experiments are conducted on the Indian and Russian borders, and in my mind's eye I have seen thousands of birds die in the course of these tests. Why these tests are being conducted in that specific area is unknown to me. I do know, though, that as a result of these experiments we will have a germ war in the future. It will be a costly war, both in loss of lives and destruction to crops.

TODAY'S YOUTH WILL REAP A BITTER HARVEST

It has been revealed to me that the new generation—those up to thirty years of age today—who neglect spiritual values will suffer untold misery. This neglect will cause them to place emphasis on the decadent aspects of our society and will result in blinding them to seeing God's purpose for them in this world.

Parents should place great importance on creating a family life that will nourish and encourage spirituality in their children. Only a turn to God and His Purpose can save them. This early training will also strengthen them against the false Oriental religious philosophy that will be moving into the Western world in the years 2020–2030. This new Oriental faith will have such a profound influence upon the Christian world that only by reaching far back into their early beliefs will Christians be able to retain their faith.

TAXES SOAR

Within the next fifteen years individual income taxes will have become such an overpowering burden on the people of America that to many it will appear as though we have regressed into the Middle Ages where every man was taxed for all of his possessions. It will not create a revolt but will greatly decrease our economic efficiency.

PSYCHIC PHENOMENA WILL INCREASE

Before the completion of the next decade, popularity of

ESP and psychic phenomena will reach an all-time high. No longer will people be inhibited by what others may say about it; they will have reached the age of experimentation in psychic matters and will probe its depths to discover the power of spirituality. Many will find faith in the Lord through ESP.

A WOMAN PRESIDENT

I feel the women of the United States will push for what they term "equality" and will go all out to succeed. Too, I see where one woman in particular will push long and hard —and with such assurance and conviction that *she will become our first woman President in the United States*. This could and will happen in the not too distant future—timing is difficult to get, but I feel it will surely be in the 1980's.

ETHEL KENNEDY REMARRIED

Ethel Kennedy, whom I greatly admire, will remarry—her bridegroom is someone she has known for a while. However, she will always be a member of the "Kennedy clan" because of her children, and she will remain politically active in very much the same way as she did when Senator Kennedy was alive.

SECOND MARRIAGE FOR STREISAND

Barbra Streisand is a "natural" in her profession. She will eventually reach out to other countries, always working diligently to improve her voice.

Her second marriage will be more successful than her first. I get that her first marriage was a bit impulsive.

Her many friends will prove taxing on both her time and her money; however, she will continue on to many more professional successes. A word of caution: As the years go by, she should watch her money and investments carefully!

A "NEW" SINATRA ABOUT TO EMERGE

Frank Sinatra has excellent mystical vibrations—but also practical thoughts pertaining to some political movement. He will write a leading article for an outstanding periodical and will weave his own personal views and philosophies into this article. I get that this will be well received nationally.

Also, he is a "natural" for the political organization, which he favors. One strong word of caution: his fortune could melt away almost before his very eyes if he is not careful.

Mr. Sinatra is very religious—has devout faith within his soul—but manages to hide it from his public.

NEW PROFESSION FOR BISHOP PIKE

Bishop Pike is a brilliant man, but the "natural" channel for him is not the channel of clergy, but the channel of a man who would be absolutely uncanny—in fact, a genius—as a medical diagnostician.

He has a great love for science and all truths. He will eventually become successful in another field.

Bishop Pike has a keen and penetrating knowledge of human nature, also a significant power of "the eye"—a sort of natural hypnotic power, one he will and does use for good, as he is able to convince people to listen to logic and reason.

I feel the people around him will take much from Bishop Pike but give little in return. Fortunately, I see that he will lose his frustrations in his new vocation.

KING CONSTANTINE AND QUEEN ANNE-MARIE OF GREECE

I get that this royal couple are having marital discord and will separate.

LYNDON JOHNSON GROWING IN STATURE

While Lyndon Baines Johnson was in the White House, I tried to warn him repeatedly that his dependence on his advisers would be his downfall. He was trapped in the Vietnamese war and remained trapped during his administration because of injudicious informants who continued to counsel him to ignore the Russian role in Vietnam. I tried to warn him not to have his meeting with Kosygin at Glassboro, for Kosygin was only a front and had no power of decision. President Johnson struggled valiantly and worked diligently to perform his presidential duties, but his supporting cast was not loyal.

He will make a greater mark on history as an elder statesman than he made as President because he now understands that it is better to be himself than to try to live in the image of another. He is now free to develop his own abilities to the full—and this he will do.

ECUMENICAL MOVEMENT

Unfortunately, the ecumenical movement, of which I expected so much, has become more of an empty dream than a workable reality. I see more trouble in the churches in this century than ever before. The coming twenty-nine years will be years of strife and division. There will be a greater understanding of each other's points of view, but it is this understanding that will make the churches realize that they are too divided to become one without divine intervention. This intervention will take place at the end of this century, when a Cross will appear in the Eastern sky and a great voice from heaven will call all men to unite under one God. Then, even though they will still remain as separate churches, they will be called to unite in one Apostolic faith and to recognize the same all-powerful God. Once again, however, many who hear God's call will not respond.

ELECTION CHANGES IMMINENT

Internal power struggles between major factions of our political parties as well as grass-roots demand for fundamental changes will completely revise our present-day system of electing our Presidents. I see a body of men and some women appoint our President and all those who occupy high office. Since this will largely curtail the power and influence of labor union leaders, it will lead to a general reorganization of all labor unions in the United States.

CARDINALS REPLACE POPE

During this century one pope will suffer bodily harm. Another will be assassinated. The assassination will be the final blow to the office of the Holy See. This pope will be the same one who will be chosen in the not too distant future but whose election will not be approved by the Roman clergy. His influence, however, will be such that he will win out over the objections of his opponents. While this pope will be the last one ever to reign as singular head of the Church, the beginnings of this change will occur with one of his predecessors who will give far-reaching power to his cardinals. These same cardinals will use their powers to replace him with one more to their liking.

THE RED CHINESE MENACE

The biggest danger the world faces in the future is Red China. When peace negotiations have been seemingly concluded in the first quarter of the twenty-first century, Red China will show her teeth.

In the year 2025 Red China will have reached an economic and political stability sufficient to forge ahead and become the Great Conqueror.

In that year Red China will march into Russia, conquer a large part of the U.S.S.R's northern area, and will not stop until it has moved into Finland, Norway, Sweden, and Denmark, stopping at the German border. It will not invade Western Europe. By that time, however, Russia will also have expanded her direct sphere of influence. It will no longer be limited to the countries of Eastern Europe but will now include Libya, Ethiopia, Iran, and much of Africa.

This war of conquest will last from 2025–2037.

MAJOR ARMED CONFLICTS IN THE MAKING

The Vietnamese war, compared to wars I see in the future, is but a small bonfire. For years now the arms for these wars have been moving into countries of the Middle East, Africa, and South America, and countries such as Venezuela, Bolivia, and Guatemala have to be watched carefully.

INTERVENTION BY NATURE

Sometime around the middle of the 1980's—in fact, I feel that it will be in the year 1985—nature will interfere with the Soviet plan for world conquest. In that year there will be a natural phenomenon which will cause profound changes in the events shaping the course of humanity—a natural phenomenon of the first order. It will shake many cynics and doubters who will turn to Christ. It will change many things, yet when it is all over, there will be large numbers of people who will refuse to admit that it ever happened.

A DECADE OF ADVANCEMENT IN THE MATERIAL WORLD

* Spurred on by excessive pressure of those who seek to destroy us, the United States will produce new sophisticated armament more advanced than that of our enemies.

* A major breakthrough in the field of propulsion—using magnetic and cosmic forces—will enable us to travel to far-off planets with a simplicity never before thought possible.

* Great changes in medicine and welfare will facilitate our health, economy, and way of life.

* Riches and food from the oceans will greatly affect our diets.

* Materials will be produced with vastly improved properties, conducting, semi-conducting, insulating, magnetic, and structural.

* Mounting energy demands will be met through the use of chemical, thermal, electro-magnetic, terman-ionic, and cosmic sources that will be harnessed.

* Electronics will advance beyond the wildest imagination. Over the past decade micro-miniaturization has advanced from 7000 parts per cubic foot to 700,000. *By 1978 this micro-miniaturization will have reached 7,000,000 components per cubic foot!*

* Educational institutions will review their curricula toward stimulating increased excellence in education, so as to develop the brain power needed by this new technology.

Let me repeat that many of the tormenting events which have been recorded here are man-made—they need not occur —but they will occur unless men turn to God.

Regardless of what our future holds for us, therefore, we should have faith in Him to continue moving assuredly forward in our individual lives. Our country is in more grave danger now than at any other time in our history. Much of the danger comes from within, created by our quest for materialistic goals and our apathy to danger. For many years, protected by the freedoms bequeathed us by our forefathers, and the great oceans that flank our shores, we have lived in security and abundance as bombs, fire, and atomic destruction have rained on other peoples.

But our protection is no longer what it used to be.

The seas around us are no longer a fast barrier against atomic missiles from the air or sea.

It behooves us to pause and consider why we are here and where we are going, so we may chart the positive course to travel in order to achieve the greater structure and the broader horizon without which we may well be lost.

Those who lack a sense of destiny and foresight may feel time shortens dimensions and direction. But those who have faith in Him will welcome every new discovery and every new experience that provides further insight into the countless, limitless wonders of His kingdom.

9

The Coming of the Antichrist

When you live in Washington, a "midsummer night's dream" is sometimes completely out of the question. Here the summers are hot and humid, and the slowly passing hours of a sleepless night make the drenching humidity even more oppressing.

The night of July 14, 1952, was one of those nights.

I had been in bed for hours and felt continuously on the threshold of waking and sleeping, that in-between stage when the subconscious works overtime and the conscious lies dormant, waiting for the rays of the early morning sun.

Suddenly I sensed something moving to the right of my bed. I felt a powerful presence moving closer to me . . .

I lay completely still, tuning my entire being into the awareness of what was happening. Then another feeling engulfed me; it was the awareness of God's love that had enveloped me to protect me from whatever was to take place.

I looked toward the foot of my bed and saw the "other" presence, shaped like a serpent, nudge gently against the mattress. I felt the pressure of its body increase, but it was the impact of a mental force which made me realize that it was not just a reptile. Powerful waves of intellect and majesty radiated from it; it was a mind that somehow "took" by "giving."

I remember thinking, "What power! What intellect! Yet it is no bigger than a garden hose."

I observed the force of its body as it moved, attempting to wrap itself around my legs and hips, but I was insulated against physical contact with it, protected from all harm to body or soul by the presence of God's protective love.

Slowly now the entire reptile presented its full self. It had grown to the size of an arm and was strikingly hued in an unusual black-and-yellow pattern.

I took a closer look at its head. Its eyes were gazing fixedly toward the East, but what made it stand out were its jowls, shaped like miniature pyramids . . .

The serpent turned its head and our eyes met. It eyes reflected all the wisdom and suffering of the ages, but also an unspoken plea for trust and understanding.

It moved its head again, facing the East once more, as if to tell me that I must look to the East for wisdom and understanding. Somehow I sensed that it was conveying to me that if my trust and faith in it were great enough, I would be able to partake of its unlimited, unearthly wisdom.

The serpent looked back, and while I gazed deeply into its eyes, it withdrew and vanished. . . .

An unusual ray of purplish light that followed the serpent in through the east window faded out as he disappeared.

I turned and looked at the dial on my bedside clock. The time was 3:14 A.M.

The vision was over.

Many times since then my mind has wandered back to that night and what I experienced. I knew, however, that to have a full understanding of the importance of this vision, a thorough knowledge of the religious value of the snake, or serpent as the Bible refers to it, was a prerequisite.

From the very moment God created the angels, the Bible teaches, He put every one of them to a test, involving some form of moral responsibility, to prove their worthiness of heaven.

Many of the angels, with the one who was to be called Satan at their head, were unwilling to use their free will rightly and committed sin against God in this test and fell from His grace. They erred through the spiritual sin of pride. They were proud of their beautiful angelic natures and powerful intellects.

At the same time the Bible teaches that the majority of the angels remained faithful to God under the leadership of Michael, and this sets the stage for a mysterious conflict between the powers of light and darkness that casts its shadow over the entire human family.

It has been a common belief among men of all tribes and peoples, since the earliest recorded times, that God has an adversary who leads all those who choose sin and evil. More interesting, however, is that scientists who researched the myths and legends of contemporary and ancient tribes have discovered *that these people still expect a final battle between God and a dragon-like monster.*

It is relevant to note that the Bible teaches a similar doctrine. In Revelation 12:7–9, St. John writes:

"And there was a battle in heaven, Michael and his angels battled with the dragon, and the dragon fought and his angels. And they did not prevail, neither was their place found anymore in heaven. And that great dragon was cast down, the ancient serpent, who is called the devil and Satan, who leads astray the whole world; and he was cast down to the earth and with him his angels were cast down."

Satan operates here on earth in many different forms and through individual human lives. He began his work on earth when, as the Old Testament reports, Eve was tempted by him, disguised as a serpent.

As she looked into the eyes of the serpent, something fascinated her with overpowering force. She saw some sort of perversely attractive wisdom and glamour there and, desiring it, fell into illusion and deception.

When Jesus met with stiff resistance to His plan of redemption from the people who were living when He walked the earth, He unmasked Satan with the plainest kind of speech.

"If God were your Father," He said in John 8:42–44, *"you would surely love me. For from God I came forth and have come. . . . Why do you not understand my speech? Because you cannot listen to my words. The father from whom you are is the devil, and the desires of your father it is your will to do. He was a murderer from the beginning, and has not stood in the truth because there is no truth in him. When he tells a lie he speaks from his very nature for he is a liar and the father of lies."*

Thus, the first and most important part of my vision of the serpent was clarified. There was no doubt that the scholars were right when they asserted that "the serpent among Christians is nothing else than the symbol of Satan, whose head will be crushed by the Son of Man when He comes."

For the Christian, the serpent, the dragon of the Bible, is linked directly with the figure of the Antichrist (a man, a "prince of peace," who will appear on the world scene claiming to be Christ), who will be one of the several signs of the second coming of Christ.

Significant in this respect is the familiar statue of the Virgin Mary standing in victory, with her feet treading on the serpent, lying helpless under her feet.

Since the entrance of Satan into this world, numerous cults with Satan-worship as their central attraction have developed. It is a phenomenon found everywhere on earth, reaching far back into prehistoric times.

Scientists who research these facts report that the cult of the serpent exists in many forms, all of them tracing back to the worship of actual serpents. However, standing behind or within the form of the serpent there has always been some inhabitant of the spirit world, a demon of sorts.

Many people have always been fascinated by the brilliance and power of the serpent's eye, the sudden, fatal consequences of its bite or its enveloping fold adding to its mystery.

Thus, the serpent became a fit subject for innumerable myths. Sometimes it was looked upon as the revealer of the arts and sciences of civilization; but always there was a connection between the serpent and a fascinating wisdom that man seeks, something other than that true and perfect wisdom which is of God.

Throughout Africa the serpent is worshiped either for itself or as the embodiment of a god. Serpent-worship extends from primitive times to the present and has carried over into the voodoo of Central America, Brazil, and Haiti.

Not only have Satan and the serpent become practically synonymous and interchangeable in religious traditions of the Christians and the Hebrews, but the heathen world has also accepted this connection.

Could there be in this Christian era a more direct identification with the ancient serpent than Satanism? There have always been mutterings of a tradition carried forth through the centuries of outright devil worship, sometimes connected with serpent-worship.

Historical records show that the King of Poland in the fourteenth century had a large number of snakes killed, which were being adored in secret and underground cults in various sections of his country. And then there are the secret rites by which Satan is worshiped in Christian times under the form of the so-called Black Mass. This is a perverted celebration, carried out as a caricature of the Holy Mass, the sacred center of the Catholic religion.

These things exist in our own times, and in the coming years this cult of Satanism will reveal itself more daringly and openly than ever before.

The Detroit *Free Press*, Thursday, May 25, 1967, carried the following news item.

Headlined "SORCERER BAPTIZES DAUGHTER," the story read as follows:

"A well-proportioned brunette tiptoed through a hushed room, decorated with a stuffed rat, two crows and a skull. She took off her clothes and lay down on a leopard skin covering a mantle. All was ready for the baptism of a child.

"Anton Szandor Lavey, who calls himself a sorcerer and the High Priest of the First Church of Satan, baptized his gum-chewing 3-year-old daughter, as a hooded organist played the 'Hymn to Satan.'

"The child, Zeena Galatea Lavey, sat quietly near the feet of the naked woman who formed the altar for the anti-religious ceremony.

"Her father, who claims to have 250 followers in San Francisco and 5,000 throughout the world, was robed and wore a hood that bore the horns of Satan. He said the mystic ceremony was the first such baptism in history."

In a more recent interview Mr. Lavey explained some of the beliefs of his "church."

"Through Satanism man's rightful place in nature is refound," he stated. "We are no longer supplicating weaklings groveling in the dust and beseeching 'God' to throw us a crumb of mercy. As sorcerers and sorceresses, we are strong. With our power and knowledge we now command our god, Satan. The Satanist worships nature in its majesty, for by doing so he sanctifies himself and his natural humanity.

"As a Satanist," he continued, "you will learn to indulge in the so-called seven deadly sins as they all lead to physical or mental gratification and were only invented by the Christian church to insure guilt on the part of their followers, as it would be impossible for anyone to avoid committing these sins.

"If you have frustrated your desires too long simply because our self-righteous society frowns upon these acts, join us! You might be surprised at the new life that will open up for you. Satan welcomes you who are alive and glad of it! *Regie Satanas.*"

It has been reported that Mr. Lavey's wife is presently putting the finishing touches to a Satanic Bible, while correspondence courses in Satanism are ready to be mailed out.

Some theologians hold that when *this* takes place, the world will be ripe for the coming of the forerunner, the "prophet" of the Antichrist. This, they claim, will lead to the most refined form of idolatry, man's worship of himself, but he will not realize that it is actually Satan, the serpent, he is worshiping.

As the prophet of the Antichrist advances his ideology, men will become dazzled by the progress of civilization and be blinded by the rich standard of living. Society will worship itself and praise its own technological advances. "*I am* power and have no need of God," many will say. "My human knowledge is sufficient for me."

This, I feel, is the essential seduction by which Satan manipulates man and draws him into a false worship of himself.

Satan showed himself to me as a serpent. I saw the wisdom of the ages reflected in its eyes; I saw the battle Eve fought—and lost—when she came face to face with it; I watched the emotions and recollections of suffering and weariness fight for my attention and understanding, but I also saw its eyes beg for faith and trust. Because of my faith in and love of God and His shielding presence I did not respond to its plea . . . and when the serpent left I still was one with God.

Satan is now coming into the open to seduce the world and we should be prepared for the inevitable events that are to follow. *I have seen that the United States is to play a major role in this development,* for as the conflict between God and Satan reaches a decisive stage, it will manifest itself here through open warfare between the forces of the Antichrist —the one who claims that *he* is the Christ but is not—and the followers of the true Christ.

The leading role of the United States in this tragedy has been made clear to me in recent visions and revelations.

The nation was led to a new philosophy in 1960 when the youth of America were told that we were to have a "new frontier" and that as part of this new frontier the youth had to become more conscious of their responsibilities and rights in our present society. Youth accepted the challenge and tried to create a "new frontier." No one, however, in 1960 asked the question, "Are they ready for this awesome responsibility?" This should have been asked before this task was delegated. They were not ready for this responsibility, but the Communist-front organizations were and guided the hordes of unprepared, destiny-seeking adolescents and their bearded brothers to use the weapons of protest. Being able to fan racial unrest and violence was not enough; now the Communists had the opportunity to infiltrate the youth organizations of America, and this they did!

The bitter irony of it all is that these young people do not realize that they are the victims, not the victors. They are forced into the battle for personal freedom, yet they do not know how to handle this privilege and are destroying and overthrowing the heritage of our country in their youthful but wild quest for power to assert and impose their false doctrines of reform.

So our country has become a battleground between the ideologies of the social order and that of the adolescents, but this is only the beginning of the trouble facing us.

I have seen a "government within a government" develop in the United States within the last few years. Political families have always contributed significantly to the development of this nation. They each spawned their own "political machine" and often used it wisely. The Roosevelts, the Rockefellers, the Lodges, the Kennedys, all had and have their influence on our country's destiny.

However, I "see" this "government within a government" being controlled and financed by the well-oiled political "machine" of one of our leading political families. With their eyes on the White House, I see them discredit any man who occupies it without their approval, no matter how good his political programs may be.

They will—through political intimidation, propaganda, and illegal sixth-column activities—make every effort to show the nation that only their man, the one who heads their "machine," has the sole right to occupy the White House. Their campaign is going to cause great harm to our nation both here and abroad.

I "see" this group succeed in taking over de facto control of the country. They will give rise to an upheaval in our social structure as never before seen. They will bring about increased racial unrest and great discontent. Foreign subversive elements will—as they did in the 1960's—infiltrate the unruly factions and cause renewed fighting on the nation's campuses and in racial ghettos.

All of the evil in the masses will be swept toward an unknown frenzy by this "machine."

I "see" a member of this "machine" ascend to power in New York City, enforcing new laws and regulations which will affect many households of that great metropolis.

The social and religious chaos generated by this political machine throughout the United States will prepare the nation for the coming of the prophet of the Antichrist. This political unit of the East will be the tool of the serpent in delivering the masses to him.

In the book of Revelation, Chapter 13:11–15, St. John describes some of the signs and duties of the prophet of the Antichrist.

"And I saw another beast coming up out of the earth," he writes, *"and it had two horns like those of a lamb, but it spoke as does a dragon. And it exercised all the authority of the former beast in its sight; and it made the earth and the inhabitants therein to worship the first beast, whose deadly wound was healed. And it did great signs, so as even to make fire come down from heaven upon earth in the sight of mankind. And it leads astray the inhabitants of the earth, by reason of the signs which it was permitted to do in the sight of the beast, telling the inhabitants of the earth to make an*

image to the beast . . . and to cause that who ever should not worship the image of the beast should be killed."

His domain will be the intellectual seduction of mankind. It means a mixture of political, philosophical, and religious ideology that will throw the populations of the world into a deep crisis of faith in God.

The idea of a forerunner or prophet is not new. Jesus had as His immediate forerunner John the Baptist, last of the Old Testament prophets, and His First Coming was prepared by a long line of those earlier prophets from Moses through Isaiah, Jeremiah, Daniel, Elijah, and others.

From all I have read concerning the coming of this prophet of the false Christ, I feel the following points are worth repeating (and remembering!):

As official forerunner, one of his first duties and responsibilities in readying the world for the advent of his "master" is to manipulate the available propaganda machines. With teaching and propaganda the prophet will cause people not merely to accept the Antichrist but rather to desire him with positive enthusiasm, to create the conditions of his coming and to participate actively in organizing the frightful and terrifying despotism of his World Empire.

Secondly, there will be "miracles," the signs and wonders that will "lead astray the inhabitants of the earth." His most convincing sign will be the conquest of the powers of nature, of which the "fire from heaven" is the ultimate symbol. These will not be supernatural or preternatural events, but rather the prodigies of science and human achievements, but interpreted in such a way as to lead men away from God and toward the worship of the Antichrist.

Thirdly, the ideological and falsely scientific prophet will develop the image of a proud and haughty spirit of anti-Christian science that will seem to make many religous traditions outmoded and unacceptable for men of what will be called that "enlightened" day. It is this image that many men will adore . . .

Fourthly and finally, there will be the period of full victorious reign of the Antichrist and his prophet. This will be the triumph of the Antichrist on the stage of universal history, and standing beside him will be the prophet, who personifies anti-Christian science. *The prophet of the Antichrist and the Antichrist himself, therefore, will be specific and identifiable persons!*

With his world-wide propaganda the prophet will teach this atheistic thinking of the apostasy from God as the unique source of all knowledge and wisdom. He will promise to bring the reign of justice upon this earth. He will offer complete liberation to mankind and will hold out the prospect of unity and solidarity, of peace and happiness among all men.

The prophet will herald a human wisdom, deeply human, all *too* human, confined to this world alone. He will entice and seduce millions to worship the works of man's own hand, to worship his own self, and ultimately to worship the Antichrist.

The prophet will communicate to men through his world propaganda machine the supreme ambitions of human science. He will announce that science is able to penetrate all of the secrets of nature, to domesticate all of the forces of nature, especially those of life, indeed of human life itself! He will profess that men will be able to live as they please, so long as they please, and to die as and when they please—and all without suffering—if they will only follow him.

In all this he will be aided and encouraged by the corrupt political machinations of the politically powerful group previously mentioned.

But this is only the introduction of what is to come. Next on the scene will be the Antichrist himself.

Who *is* the Antichrist?

From the account of human origin in the book of Genesis, Chapter 3, it is clear that sin and evil became a reality *and* a problem in human affairs from the very beginning. God, however, at the same time, promised to send His Anointed One to establish the Kingdom of God among men, with the promise of final and complete victory over the powers of sin and evil. Yet, even though the time and circumstances of Christ's *First Coming* were indicated in precise and exact details, it was easy to overlook it as it took place in a most humble and lowly way, hidden from public view and not manifested by an immense sign forcing itself upon men from on high.

His *Second Coming* will be marked by signs of His majesty.

"And when He had said this, He was lifted up before their eyes, and a cloud took Him out of their sight. And while they were gazing up to heaven as He went, behold, two men stood by them in white garments, and said to them, 'Men of Galilee, why do you stand looking up to heaven? This Jesus who has been taken up from you into heaven will come in the same way you have seen him going up to heaven.'" (Acts of the Apostles 1:9–11.)

The Second Coming of Christ will signify the end of sin and the end of the reign of the serpent. The rule of Satan, consequently, will be one of deception. He will make every effort to have humanity accept *him* as their savior.

Each book of the Bible makes its own kind of contribution toward this Christian certitude that Jesus will come again.

Christ Himself gave the reason for this over and over again.

"For what does it profit a man, if he gain the whole world, but suffers the loss of his own soul? Or what will a man give in exchange for his soul? For the Son of Man is to come with His angels in the glory of His Father, and then He will render to everyone according to his conduct." (Matthew 16:26–27.)

Thus the doctrine of the Second Coming of Christ became an absolute truth in the Christian faith.

How much time will expire between the arrival of the Antichrist and the Second Coming of Christ no one knows

. . . *"not even the Angels of heaven, but the Father only."* (Matthew 24:36.)

"But in those days, after that tribulation, the sun will be darkened and the stars of heaven will be falling, and then they will see the Son of Man coming upon the clouds with great power and mystery." (Mark 13:24–26.)

Christ has given us ample warning as to when we might expect the arrival of the Antichrist. In fact, He gives numerous signs by which the coming of the Antichrist may be anticipated. There will be disturbances of various kinds in nature and especially in society, upheavals and revolutions that break up and overthrow the order of things. There will be, as interpreted by many, the conversion of Israel to accept Christ. But the greatest of the signs will be the acceptance of a false religion, and finally the manifestation of the Antichrist.

The Antichrist will be a phenomenon of the political order. He is not simply a religious "heretic" whom the world at large could safely ignore. No! He will hold earthly power in his hands and use it as his instrument. All the tyrants of history are mere children in comparison with him.

This means first of all that he will be a military figure beyond anything the world has ever previously seen. He will conquer the whole earth and hold it in complete mastery with the most modern weapons. He will rule his new World Empire with the utmost of military might and glory.

Furthermore, the Bible prophecies make it intelligible that the World Empire of the Antichrist will be a totalitarian state in the most extreme meaning of the word. He will exercise power over the entire world and each person intensively, controlling even his thoughts. There will be no "neighboring state," and the whole world will become an island within the universe. War as it has been known will fade away, and the Antichrist will announce himself as the "prince of peace."

For the Christian church, however, I see no relief. The church will ultimately have only one place to go—underground. Nothing will remain of the distinguished position it enjoyed as the leader and sponsor of human culture; nothing will be left of its institutional power, yet the Holy Spirit will remain with the church as Christ revealed: ". . . to the end of time."

But I foresee something deeper in the coming godless social order of the Antichrist, something more than mere political system, something that reaches into the fallen condition of human nature. *He will establish and lead a strange and fundamentally anti-human "religion" of atheism and anti-religion.*

Referring to the beast that Christian tradition understands to be the Antichrist, Revelation 13:7 states, *"There was given to it authority over every tribe, and people, and tongue and nation."* So there is more involved here than the mere political authority of a World Empire!

I see two definite characteristics distinguishing the Antichrist: dominion over men with a rod of iron and seduction of their minds by a false ideology and propaganda. He will present himself to all mankind as the supreme ruler who stills and quells all warfare on earth, as the teacher of man's new modernized approach to life that leaves the Christian heritage behind as outmoded, and as the "redeemer" of all men from their old fears, guilt complexes, and mistreatment of each other.

He will be the exact opposite of Christ. He will be His adversary and at the same time appear to be His imitator.

Christians who have studied this coming see him in the light of Biblical prophecy as a perverted imitation-Christ, posing with a deceptive appearance of good will, religiosity, and even holiness. He will seem to be a religious figure, offering to men a strangely twisted fulfillment of their spiritual desires. There will be more here than just the wearing of a cloak as disguise. The Antichrist will be a deeply ethical challenge to the human masses of his time, almost forcing them to admit his "holiness," precisely because those human masses will no longer be able to comprehend and recognize the original meaning of "holiness" in human life and worship. This is the result of what atheism will do to them.

Despite his religiosity and appearance of humanism, however, the Antichrist will in actuality be an atheist.

"Who is a liar but he that denieth that Jesus is the Christ? He is anti-christ, that denieth the Father and the Son." (I John 2:22.)

The atheism, which the Bibilical prophets anticipated concerning the Antichrist, becomes even more visible when we consider that they described him as the object of idolatrous worship on the part of mankind. He will be the last and the greatest of idols man has worshiped in the long history of religious aberrations. He will receive the worship of many people, as if he, in his own person, were actually God. He will personify, in other words, a false humanism by which men worship themselves, making of themselves their own supreme law, and finding in the Antichrist the symbol of the secret aspiration of their own fallen natures. . . .

But since he will set himself up as a god before all men and will demand *worship* of *all* men, he will not tolerate worship of the one true God. Hence he will wage a full, unbridled persecution of all Christians.

From the very beginning of Christianity its followers have expected that the coming of the Antichrist would be accompanied by fierce persecution. Using the words of the prophet Daniel, Jesus said:

"For then there will be great tribulation, such as has not been from the beginning of the world to this time, no, nor ever shall be.

"And except those days should be shortened, there should no flesh be saved: but for the elect's sake those days shall be shortened." (Matthew 24:21-22.)

This demoniac deception that will force itself upon mankind in those days will have two main components: (1) a false ideology pressed upon the minds of men by world-wide propaganda; (2) mysterious signs and wonders. As Jesus the Messiah worked divine miracles to prove the authenticity of His mission, so the Antichrist, the false Messiah, through Satanic power, will offer mankind "proof" of his "authenticity."

Cardinal Newman, describing the infiltration of ideas that is to eventuate when we reach the approximate arrival time of the prophet of the Antichrist, has stated:

"Far be it from us to be seduced with the fair promises in which Satan is sure to hide his poison! Do you think he is so unskillful in his craft as to ask you openly and plainly to join him in the warfare against the truth? No! He offers you bait to tempt you. *He promises you civil liberty; he promises you equality; he promises you trade and wealth; he promises you a remission of taxes; he promises you reform.* This is the way in which he conceals from you the kind of work to which he is putting you; he tempts you to rail against your rulers and superiors; he does so himself, and induces you to imitate him; or he promises you illumination. He offers you knowledge, science, philosophy and enlargement of mind. He scoffs at times gone by; he scoffs at every institution that reveres them."

As a result of the powerful influence and persuasion of the prophet of the Antichrist, universal confusion, division, and schisms will prevail. Some religions will change into heathenism, and the remnant, the faithful few, who will retain their belief in the one true God will suffer great violence— and all as a result of the works of the so-called "prince of peace."

"For they will deliver you up to councils," Jesus foretells, *"and you will be beaten in synagogues, and you will stand before governors and kings for my sake, be a witness to them . . . Do not be anxious beforehand what you are to speak; but speak whatever is given you in that hour. For it is not you who are speaking, but the Holy Spirit. And brother will hand over brother to death, and the father his child; children*

will rise up against parents, and put them to death. And you will be hated by all for my name's sake; but he who has persevered to the end will be saved." (Mark 13:9–13.)

St. John goes even further and predicts in Revelation 13: 15–17, *". . . that the image of the beast should both speak and cause that whoever should not worship the image of the beast should be killed. And it will cause all, the small and the great, the rich and the poor, the free and the bond, to have a mark on their right hand or on their foreheads, and it will bring about that no one will be able to buy or sell, except him who has the mark, either the name of the beast or the number of its name."*

So there will be economic sanctions for those who will not cooperate with the Antichrist.

Pondering these prophecies and others like them in the Bible, Cardinal Newman commented sadly, "This persecution will be worse than any persecution before it."

Such, then, is the figure of the Antichrist that Biblical prophecies foresee.

More and more do I see our destiny as a nation intertwined with the events shaping the coming of this fearful personage.

Why did God lift the veil of the future and permit us to see the outlines of the "last days"? He did it because He loves us and wants each one of us to prepare ourselves—to set our goals and chart our courses—for what is to come.

10

The Child From the East

A revelation that was given me on the morning of February 5, 1962, and partly reported in *A Gift of Prophecy*, foretells one of the most dramatic events in the history of the world.

If our world is "a lesson book for the universe," as some have said, then the event that is foreshadowed in this prophecy should be one of the most instructive chapters in the history of man.

Invariably, at the termination of my speeches, when I indicate my desire to answer listeners' questions, people ask me for more details regarding the child that was the focal point of this prophecy.

"When," they ask, "will we hear more about him? Where is he now? When will he make his appearance on the world scene?"

I feel the time has come to report the revelation in its entirety.

It began on the evening of February 2, 1962, when, while meditating in my room, I became aware of a curious phenomenon. The lights grew dim, and as I looked up at the chandelier I noticed all five bulbs darken, except for a curious round ball of brilliance which glowed in the center of each. It did not last long. In fact, I recall thinking that it was probably caused by some defect in the electrical system.

Jimmy felt the same way and both of us forgot about the "light failure" until the same phenomenon reoccurred the following evening.

Again I was meditating, seeking our Lord. This time the light faded out a second time, leaving only those brilliant globes of light within. How much time elapsed exactly I do not know—perhaps ten seconds—but I suddenly became cognizant of a tiny crackling sound emanating from inside the globes. When the crackling sound ceased, the lights returned to normal. I then began to sense something was happening over which I had no control. When, however, the performance was repeated in exactly the same manner on the third evening, I knew that an event of tremendous importance was about to be revealed to me. I then realized that the phenomenon of the lights was a prelude of things to come.

I went to bed, confident that God would let me know if and when I was to receive this revelation.

He did.

It happened early the following morning, on the fourth day, when I awoke and walked toward the east window of my room, preparing to greet our Lord with the Twenty-third Psalm on my lips.

I gazed out my window and, although the sun was still in hiding, what I saw was almost beyond description.

The bare-limbed trees of the city had given way to an endless desert scene, broiled by a relentless sun. Glowing like an enormous ball of fire, the sun had cracked the horizon, emitting brilliant rays of scintillating light which seemed to attract the earth like a magic wand.

The sun's rays parted, facilitating the appearance of an Egyptian Pharaoh and his queen. I immediately recognized her as Queen Nefertiti; the man with her I took to be her husband, reported by history to be Ikhnaton, the so-called "heretic Pharaoh." Holding hands as lovers do, they emerged from the brilliant rays, majestic in their bearing; Ikhnaton's royal headdress was a sign of his power under the sun . . . not of power under the Son.

But my eyes were drawn to Nefertiti and the child she tenderly cradled in her other arm. It was a newborn babe, wrapped in soiled, ragged swaddling clothes. He was in stark contrast to the magnificently arrayed royal couple.

Not a sound broke the unearthly silence as they issued forth with the child. I then became aware of a multitude of people that appeared between the child and me. It seemed as though the entire world was watching the royal couple present the baby. Watching the baby over their heads, I witnessed Nefertiti hand the child to the people. Instantly rays of sunlight burst forth from the little boy, carefully blending themselves with the brilliance of the sun, blotting out everything but him.

Ikhnaton disappeared from the scene. Nefertiti remained. I observed her walking away from the child and the people, into the past, into the secret past of the ancients. Thirsty and tired, she rested beside a water jug, and just as she cupped her hands to drink, a sudden thrust of a dagger in her back ended her life. Her death scream, piercing and mournful, faded out with her.

My eyes once more focused on the baby. By now he had grown to manhood, and a small cross which had formed above his head enlarged and expanded until it covered the earth in all directions. Simultaneously, suffering people, of all races, knelt in worshipful adoration, lifting their arms and offering their hearts to the man. For a fleeting moment I felt as though I were one of them, but the channel that emanated from him was not that of the Holy Trinity. I knew within my heart that this revelation was to signify the beginning of wisdom, but *whose* wisdom and for *whom?* An overpowering feeling of love surrounded me, but the look I had seen in the man when he was still a babe—a look of serene wisdom and knowledge—made me sense that here was something God allowed me to see without my becoming a part of it.

I also sensed that I was once again safe within the protective arms of my Creator.

I glanced at my bedside clock. It was still early—7:17 A.M.

What does this revelation signify? I am convinced that this revelation indicates a child, born somewhere in the Middle East shortly after 7 A.M. on February 5, 1962—possibly a direct descendant of the royal line of Pharaoh Ikhnaton and Queen Nefertiti—will revolutionize the world. There is no doubt that he will fuse multitudes into one all-embracing doctrine. He will form a new "Christianity," based on his "almighty power," but leading man in a direction far removed from the teachings and life of Christ, the Son.

As for the connection between "the child" and Ikhnaton and Nefertiti, let us examine the records of ancient Egypt.

✠✠✠✠

It was a proud and stately procession that moved slowly down the King's Way. It was sunrise and time for Ikhnaton's worship of Aton, the god of the Disk of the Sun.

His ceremonial walk in the temple procession, surrounded by his priests and accompanied by his wife, the beautiful Nefertiti, was a journey of victory. Son of Amenophis III, the most illustrious monarch of Egypt's Eighteenth Dynasty who formed historical and far-reaching alliances with the kings of Babylonia and Assyria, Ikhnaton had become seriously disenchanted with the religion of his forefathers. The god Horus had lost all attraction for him; Osiris had lost his value. He had noticed the new wind of monotheism that had begun blowing in from the fierce Habiru, a desert tribe, and he felt ill at ease with the many gods that had long preyed on the superstitions of his people. He wanted ONE god and found him in the Disk of the Sun.

Aton, the sun, was to be *his* god and, encouraged by his royal spouse, he embarked on an adventure, so daring, so "ungodly," that it made his newly appointed priests quake with fear. Not only did he decide on a more advanced form of religion, he took steps to vacate Thebes, the royal capital, and chose as the site for Aton's capital Akhetaton, a stretch of barren land located about three hundred miles north of Thebes. There, protected by steep, impregnable cliffs on three sides, he planned and built the city.

Egyptian cities dedicated to the gods were of great beauty, yet Ikhnaton managed to surpass them all. With slave labor and a multitude of captives he transformed the desert into a dream city, complete with temples, palaces, parks, and mansions.

Unknown to the powerful priests of Amon who still held most of the nation in their grip, Ikhnaton had set out on a secret expedition during the sixth year of his reign and, with a team of trusted engineers, had proceeded to stake out the district of Aton, the center of which would be his capital. Official stele (inscribed plaques) discovered in the early part of this century indicate that it took only a scant two years to ready the city for its inhabitants—and a magnificent city it turned out to be. Of the three main thoroughfares, King's Way was the most impressive one, flanked by the river on one side and by the main religious and temporal edifices on the other. There was Maru-Aton (the Palace of Pleasure), the Royal House, the Central Palace, the Great Temple of Aton, and the North Palace. Priests and high government officials were all housed on another thoroughfare that ran parallel to the King's Way. The geographical center of the city had been reserved for the Foreign Office, the National Archives, the Hall of Tribute, and the Royal Estate.

But it was the Great Temple that controlled every facet of the young monarch's activities.

Ikhnaton had chosen the Great Temple to be the "mother church" for Atonism.

Atonism was different from the old religion. True, it required a belief in many of the same doctrines, yet it focused on *one* god and disregarded most of the gods that for so long had held the Egyptians in mental bondage.

When Ikhnaton had changed his name from Amenhotep III to Ikhnaton, he did so in honor of the god Aton. His new religion was seemingly inspired and influenced by the strange people, the Habiru, who were beginning to show their hand of strength in the desert. If they were so all-powerful, Ikhnaton reasoned, could it possibly be that it had something to do with their religion that recognized only *one* God?

His religion brought about great changes in the Egyptian temple service. Gone were the sculptured images which made the Theban temples so impressive; gone were the elaborate esoteric rites. Music filled the holy places to please Aton, and secret ceremonies gave way to the ritualistic offering of food and wine. It had become a humane religion. Even his name, Ikhnaton, signified how much he believed he was doing the will of the sun-god.

"He in whom Aton [the sun-god] is satisfied" was the meaning of his name. The hieroglyphics of his name can also be translated as "He in whom the Solar Disk is satisfied." His religion had changed, but he remained a pagan, worshiping a pagan god.

At every sunrise and upon each setting of the sun, the king and queen could be seen leading a procession to the Great Temple, chanting hymns to the sun-god.

"Thy rising is beautiful in the horizon of heaven, O living Aton," he sang, according to the hieroglyphics. "Thou who givest life. Shining from the eastern horizon, Thou fillest Egypt with thy beauty . . . Thy setting is beautiful, O living Aton, who guidest all countries that they make praise at thy dawning and at thy setting."

Leaving the Great Temple and walking into the grove, accompanied by his priests, he would continue his idolatrous adoration.

"O Lord, how manifold are thy works, the whole land is in joy because of thee. All that thou hast made leaps before thee. Eyes have life at the sight of thy beauty; hearts have health when the Aton shines. There is no poverty for him who hath set thee in his heart."

For the first time during his reign Ikhnaton was happy and content, and it reflected in his family life.

Since the discovery and excavation of his city, now known as Amarna, much has been found that sheds light on his private life. Unconventional scenes in colored relief often picture Ikhnaton and Nefertiti sitting with their arms around each other. Another depicts him leaning upon a staff while Nefertiti teasingly allows him to smell a bouquet of flowers. More revealing, however, is the relief showing the queen sitting on Ikhnaton's knee.

"Happiness-in-truth" seemed to be the foundation of Ikhnaton's reign, but the frantic pursuit of this concept blinded him from the realities that confronted his nation.

In *Ancient Records of Egypt*, Professor Breasted, the eminent Egyptologist, writes that "after the victories of Thutmosis III and his immediate successors . . . a new menace to Egyptian superiority over Syria-Palestine had arisen. Among these letters (found in the old Tell el-Amarna library), most of which are addressed to Ikhnaton, there are a large number from the vassal kings to the Pharaoh which contain reiterated requests for help against the attacks of the enemies. Among these enemies were those who are called the Habiru . . . we may without hesitation adopt the conviction of the majority of experts, namely that the name is equivalent to the 'Hebrews.'"

The story of the discovery of Ikhnaton's library among the ruins of his ancient city is a fable unto itself. It happened in 1887 when an Egyptian peasant woman, digging in a field outside one of the many villages of rural Egypt, found a number of clay tablets with strange, unknown inscriptions written on them. Sensing that they might be of some value, she peddled them to a fellow villager, who in turn sold them to an antique dealer. The chain of events lengthened until the tablets finally arrived at the British Museum and the

Berlin Museum where they were immediately recognized as valuable correspondence dating back to the Eighteenth Dynasty or approximately 1400 B.C.

Professor E. A. Wallis Budge, Keeper of the Egyptian and Assyrian Antiquities of the British Museum, who rushed to Egypt and joined in the search for more clay tablets, described what transpired after his arrival. In *By Nile And Tigris,* he writes:

". . . In the course of the day, a man arrived from Hajji Kandil, bringing with him some half-dozen of the clay tablets which had been found accidentally by a woman at Tell al-'Amarnah, and he asked me to look at them and to tell him whether they were genuine or forgeries.

"When I examined the tablets I found that the matter was not as simple as it looked. In shape and form, and colour and material, the tablets were unlike anything I had ever seen in London or Paris, and the writing on all of them was of a most unusual character and puzzled me for hours. By degrees I came to the conclusion that the tablets were certainly not forgeries, and that they were neither royal annals nor historical inscriptions in the ordinary sense of the word, nor business or commercial documents. The opening words of nearly all the tablets proved them to be letters or dispatches, and I felt certain that the tablets were both genuine and of very great importance.

"I then tried to make arrangements with the men from Hajji Kandil to get the remainder of the tablets from Tell al-'Amarnah into my possession but they told me that they belonged to dealers who were in treaty with an agent of the Berlin Museum of Cairo. Among the tablets was a very large one, about 20 inches long and broad in proportion. We now know that it contained a list of the dowry of a Mesopotamian princess who was going to marry a king of Egypt. The man who was taking this to Cairo hid it between his inner garment and covered himself with his great cloak. As he stepped up into the railway coach, this tablet slipped from his clothes and fell on the bed of the railway and broke in pieces. Many natives in the train and on the platform witnessed the accident and talked freely about it and thus the news of the discovery of the tablets reached the ears of the Director of Antiquities. He at once telegraphed to the Mudir of Asyut, and ordered him to arrest and put in prison everyone who was found to be in possession of tablets, and as we have seen, he himself set out for Upper Egypt to seize all the tablets he could find."

Careful study of the more than 350 clay tablets discovered proved that the feeling that this was an exceptional find was substantiated. The documents represent the official diplomatic correspondence between kings of Egypt and their vassal rulers of the areas of Palestine, Syria, Asia Minor, Babylonia, Assyria, and various other places.

The land of Canaan at this time was to some extent under the protection of Egypt. Under enemy attack, the king of Jerusalem immediately dispatched a number of messengers to the Pharaoh and asked him to send soldiers who could help (in fighting the invading Habiru). The Pharaoh, Ikhnaton, was busy with a religious reformation. He was determined to replace the worship of many gods with that of one god, and his reform brought on his head mounting problems. He had neither the time nor desire to send troops to the king of Jerusalem.

"What he wrote him," Edward Chiera relates in *They Wrote On Clay*, "if he wrote at all, we do not know, for in those times apparently, they did not make copies of letters sent, and all we have now are the letters delivered from outside. But whether he wrote or not, the fact remains that he did not send any troops. This we can easily find out by reading a second letter from the king of Jerusalem, reiterating the previous request and warning the pharaoh that unless he makes an effort to protect his domain, the land of Canaan will be lost to him.

"The second appeal found the same reception as the first,

and in a last letter the king of Jerusalem tells him that soldiers are not needed anymore; it is too late. Much of the land has already fallen into the hands of the invaders."

A similar complaint came to Ikhnaton from Zimridi, the official in charge of Sidon. His message reads in part as follows:

". . . Your majesty should also know that the enmity against me is very great. All the towns which the king has placed under me have joined the Habiru-brigands. Would that the king place me under the protection of the man who will lead the archers of the king, so that I might reclaim the towns which have joined the Habiru-brigands, and put them under me again. Then I would be able to serve my Lord the king just as our forefathers did before."

But the king did not care to listen or reply. . . .

After Ikhnaton's death his new-found religion could no longer hold out against the powers of the priests of Amon. Territories had been lost to the Hebrews, the people who were being led by their all-powerful God. It was, in fact, the invasion by the children of God into the vassal kingdoms of the Pharaoh that helped bring about his downfall and the collapse of the false religion of the sun-god. Polytheism once again took over most of the world. The great danger of a fallacious world religion under *one* god, the sun-god, had for the time being been avoided.

How victorious his successor proved to be in eradicating Atonism is shown by his name: Tut-Ankh-Amon.

Broken-hearted, Queen Nefertiti left the Central Palace and moved into the North Palace on the outskirts of Akhetaton. Enraged priests of Amon proceeded to destroy whatever could cause even a spark of remembrance of Atonism, going so far as to completely demolish the images of the heretic Pharaoh.

Fighting together—without realizing the divine guidance behind it—the Habiru and the High Priest of Amon had accomplished what God had planned: the destruction and eradication of the Egyptian Anti-god.

The forces of love contained the forces of evil until 3328 years later, when, on February 5, 1962, Nefertiti and Ikhnaton were once more used to perpetrate this grand deception, and they again appeared on the scene, presenting their descendant to the human race.

From what I have seen of this child since his birth, I am convinced that there are too many similarities to the birth and the life of Christ to be mere coincidence. There is an unnatural planning behind the birth and function of this child. The very fact, however, that the pagan Pharaoh Ikhnaton and his wife Queen Nefertiti presented this child to the world seems to indicate that his mission is to continue where *their* first attempt to deceive humanity failed.

The circumstances surrounding the birth of the "Child of the East" and the events I have since seen taking place in his life make him appear so Christlike, yet so different, *that there is no doubt in my mind that the "child" is the actual person of the Antichrist, the one who will deceive the world in Satan's name.*

His life will seem to be an imitation of Christ's life on earth. Imitation is the most sincere form of flattery, and here Satan uses the imitation of his adversary to work his demoniac will into the lives of men.

From the little baby Jesus he borrowed the swaddling clothes and clothed his "imitation of Christ" in them before allowing Nefertiti and Ikhnaton to introduce him to the world. The question as to "why" is obvious.

In St. Luke, Chapter 2:10–12, we read:

"And the angel said unto them: Fear not: for behold, I bring you tidings of great joy, which shall be to all people.

"For unto you is born this day in the city of David a Saviour, which is Christ the Lord.

"And this shall be a sign unto you: Ye shall find the babe wrapped in swaddling clothes, lying in a manger."

Christ's message at birth was that of a loving Saviour who had come into the world to release His tortured creation from the bonds of Satan.

As I watched the little child being presented to mankind, I became strongly aware of the tremendous and compelling force that went out from him. In his eyes I found serene wisdom and unlimited knowledge, but when I "touched" his channel, I felt it was not from God.

But the birth, the introduction of the "imitation," was to be more glorious, more impressive, more illuminating in earthly terms. Thus the coming of the child was backed by the image of the rising sun, symbolizing the tremendous force at the disposal of this child who is to lead the world, but also symbolic of the false religion he is to bring with him.

The next important happening in the life of the baby Jesus came when the angel of the Lord appeared to Joseph in a dream.

". . . *saying, Arise, and take the young child and his mother, and flee into Egypt, and be thou there until I bring thee word, for Herod will seek the young child to destroy him."* (Matthew 2:13.)

A similar event has already taken place in the life of the child of my vision.

I see that he is no longer in the country where he was born but has been taken to another Middle Eastern country—I get the distinct impression that it is a densely populated area of the United Arab Republic—by his parents. Why they decided to move, I do not know. But I *do* know that there are forces working around him which are protecting him. The possibility exists that the "child" and his parents may again move to another country. I have no guarantee that his vibrations will continue to emanate from Arabia until such time as his public emergence.

We do not know much about Christ's life before the beginning of his public ministry, but there is a brief moment when,

at the age of twelve, the Bible tells us, He became aware of
His mission.

*"And when he was twelve years old, they went up to
Jerusalem after the custom of the feast . . . And he said unto
them, How is it that ye sought me? Wist ye not that I must
be about my Father's business?"* (Luke 2:42–49.)

In the following eighteen years Christ prepared Himself
for the three and a half years of His ministry on earth.

When the child reaches eleven years of age, close to twelve,
something of tremendous importance will happen to him.
We will not necessarily begin to hear about him at that time
(1973–74), but at this age he, too, will become aware of his
Satanic mission and purpose in life. He will then expand his
influence, and those around him will finally form a small
nucleus of dedicated followers when he reaches the age of
nineteen. He will work quietly with them until he is twenty-
nine or thirty years old, when the forcefulness and impact of
his presence in the world will begin to bear his forbidden
fruit.

In the same manner as Christ and His disciples spread the
Gospel, so the child and his disciples will propagate the religion of the false god. The difference will be, however, that
they will not stand alone but will have the power and the
propaganda machine of the United States backing them, advancing his cause beyond anything ever thought possible. It
will be around the time of his emergence, too, that the work
of the prophet of the Antichrist, discussed in the previous
chapter, will have reached its summit. Again, the similarity
with the Bible story concerning the life of Christ is striking,
for Christ, too, had his prophet, John the Baptist, who prepared the way for Him.

As a result of the tremendous propaganda efforts of the
prophet of the Antichrist, the influence of Christianity will
have greatly diminished by the time the seductive child is
thirty years of age. Christian education in the schools will

have come almost to a standstill, and the youth will have become extremely vulnerable to the coming of the man. I see that the youth of the world will accept him and will work closely with him in placing the world into his eager hands.

Again, the similarity with Christ cannot be denied.

". . . *Suffer little children to come unto me, and forbid them not: for of such is the kingdom of God.*

"Verily I say unto you, Whosoever shall not receive the kingdom of God as a little child shall in no wise enter therein." (Luke 18:16–17.) This was said by Christ when the disciples sought to interfere as the crowd brought forth infants to Him to be blessed.

When the "man" has reached the age reserved for the outset of his mission, no one will be able to hold the children back, *for to capture the youth and, through them, the world, the little boy was born.*

Like Christ, the Antichrist, too, will center his work around the city of Jerusalem. I get the distinct feeling that the religions of the Western world will somehow merge with the philosophies of the East. I see the youth flock to him and partake of his wisdom in much the same way that some of the youth of today make their pilgrimages to their Gurus.

With the world fully prepared for his coming, millions on our earth will be brought into contact with him through our far-advanced communications network. The Holy City will be his headquarters, but his field of labor will be the world.

Close cooperation between the then ruling powers in the United States and the new "spiritual" ruler will expose Americans to him in person as his visits here will be frequent and far reaching.

He will lead many souls astray. I saw a great crowd follow him reverently as he walked up a long road. This marked the end of his rule. In awe and filled with blind adoration, they followed him, neglecting to listen to the inner voice of the Lord that called them to repent.

I saw him stop and turn around . . . he gazed at the masses of worshipful humanity with a hypnotic look of wisdom and enticed them to follow him all the way to the end of the road. Once more he turned, and in a scene reminiscent of the "Pied Piper," he continued to lead, and the people followed him with conviction and a sense of fulfillment.

Even so, God still did not forsake them but gave them one last chance. I saw humanity arrive at the "valley of decision," a fork in the road, where the "Child of the East" slowed down as though engaged in deep thought, and with a gentle flowing of his robes made a sharp turn to the left. This moment marked the point of decision, for here everyone individually was given the choice of either veering to the left and following the child or going on, continuing to where the path became straight and narrow.

The "Pied Piper" had done his work well, for the uncountable masses followed him in quiet adoration.

I looked ahead, and the vision dissolved into utter darkness and desolation that awaited them at the end of the road.

Then I looked the other way and noticed small bands of faithful pilgrims wearily climbing their way across the obstacles that covered the narrow path. Tired and worn, but relying on their faith in the Son, they fought the last hurdle and penetrated the shield of sin that had prevented their close relationship with the Lord for so long.

They were home—finally home. Satan and the grand deception of the "Child of the East" were now only a mere page in the annals of the long war between Christ and His adversary. With victory assured, once more the universe was in harmony with its Creator.

God has revealed these things to come in order that those who believe His warning will prepare.

Some will ask, "What can one man do in the face of all these fearful prophecies?"

The answer should be obvious. Each one of us can redirect our lives from materialistic, self-seeking pleasures and moral complacency to faithful service to God, using the talents He gave us so each one of us may fulfill His purpose for us.

It is in that sense that God and one is a majority.

11

God and One Is a Majority

From the very moment we are conceived and receive life, we become a part of God—and from that instant God enriches our tiny spark of "being" with specific talents and qualities that make each one of us unique. Every new conception is a privileged creation, and He watches over each one of us from that moment of life through eternity.

Receiving life is a blessing in itself; receiving a talent of rare and unique quality is a privilege granted only by God, and no man can choose or exchange it. Only God can take it from us. He gave each one of us a talent according to our needs and His wisdom. Only He knows what is needed in a given century, and when He gives life, He creates it with the talent that the world needs at that particular time.

With this talent, however, comes the power of free will. God allows us to choose the extent to which we will develop our God-given talents. When we choose to use what He has given us, we strengthen our channels of communication with our fellow-men and with our Creator.

Only when we recognize and accept life as a unique gift, a *special* gift, and employ our individual talents to the fullest measure of our capabilities will we find harmony within ourselves, with Him and the universe. It is this balance within that determines our stature among men and before God.

When, on the other hand, we recognize but *neglect* our

talents and turn away from our appointed places in life—perhaps because we desire to be someone we are not—we resist His purpose and become frustrated and lost. We prevent our inner selves from being made manifest. Discontent and frustration become our daily companions.

There are those who regard life as an accident of birth, a freak of nature without meaning or purpose. Either they dejectedly accept their lots in life or they generate fierce determinations to get ahead at any cost. They fight for position, for rank, and for privileges—for what they call their "rights."

Still others are passive. They refuse to accept the fact that *everyone* has special talents and is capable of worthwhile accomplishments by developing his talents to the best of his abilities.

Thousands of letters pour into my office asking the same simple question:

"How can I find my natural talent?"

For those who have serious doubts about their God-given birth gift, there are tests available which reveal natural aptitudes; yet most of us need no test. We have an instinct—perhaps intuition is the better word—if we only care to listen, that will direct us to the work we can and should do.

There are those who find fascination in the columns of black and red figures in ledgers and feel that their contributions are to help maintain orderly records—only some have the talent for this work. Others yearn to teach and prepare the youth of today for the problems of tomorrow by helping them to discover and develop their individual gifts—only some have a talent for teaching. Still others are drawn to the soil with a talent to make things grow to nourish the world. Be it science, humanities, religion, or philosophy, most people have a sense of what they can and should do sometime during their lives. Too few heed the signs be they early or late, or persevere in pursuit of their purposes in life.

Once we have discovered our talents, we must knock relentlessly on *that* door which gives us access to the work for which we are gifted, never turning aside until the door has been opened, however slightly. For us to expect others to recognize our gifts and swing open the door for us to enter is unrealistic. There is no shortcut to success. There is no easy way to an immediate and brilliant career. Christ served His apprenticeship for thirty years, growing "in wisdom, age, and grace" until He was prepared to do His Father's work. We too need time for preparation, the tenure of which is determined by the providence of God and by our abilities and willingness to learn and listen.

The more faithfully we apply ourselves during this time, the richer will be the ultimate rewards.

And in this time of preparation, as in our days of fulfillment, let us pray.

* Wake up with a prayer on your lips.

* Pray while going to work, asking for strength and guidance.

* Pray when returning home, thanking Him for His help . . . and when you feel a special need of His love and strength, do not hesitate to ask for it, for He is with you always.

* Enter sleep with a prayer.

Too many people enter prayer with the idea of asking Him to do things for *them*; always asking, never truly thanking Him for all His blessings. We may need a spiritual "handout" from time to time, but we always need divine guidance for strength of character and physical endurance to live the particular lives for which He created us.

Ask for guidance to obtain a better understanding of those dear to you. Ask for guidance to obtain that degree of maturity necessary in everyday life. Ask for guidance to find out what you can give to the world, not what the world can give you.

Our acceptance of divine guidance determines our degree of dedication. Such acceptance is the only way to spiritual harmony, success, happiness, and prosperity.

I receive thousands of letters asking, "How can I find my own true channel in life—my own channel of communication with my fellow-man?"

Again, I say, pray!

Everything depends on your relationship with God. Never for one moment should we lose faith in believing that we have our own individual places in life. We all have our own approaches, our own sensitivities, our own weaknesses, and above all, our own methods of communication for sharing our innermost feelings with our fellow-men. To some it is a smile; to others it is that gentle look of understanding. Finding our channels creates peace of mind and joy of spirit that is unequaled.

Repeatedly the Bible alerts us to the importance of working with our talents. The most familiar reference is the parable in which a master, leaving on a journey, gave one servant five talents, another two, and a third, one talent. Upon his return he had praise for the first two servants who worked with and increased the talents he entrusted to them, but his displeasure with the third servant who buried his talent was so great that he took it away from him.

We too bury our talents in many different ways, through indolence, lack of initiative, defeatism, chronic depression, etc., but there is one more "burial ground" and that is fear. Not the healthy, protective fear that engulfs us with an energizing rush of adrenalin when we see a car bearing down on us or see a child trapped in the angry waves—no, such fear soon ebbs away, leaving us once again in full possession of ourselves. The fear to be feared, and to be cast out, is the one which steals into our beings to impede us with self-doubts, the fear that keeps us awake at night with its wretched whisperings, the one that smothers our strength and talents.

I recall that many years ago my husband, fearing raised eyebrows of the critics, asked me to stop using my crystal ball. But using the crystal ball was not and is not my purpose. He never doubted my psychic gift, but he did not think

the *world* would understand. He was protective, but I had
to hold on to my purpose in life, and by experience I can
tell you that holding to your purpose in life will not be easy.
But then we were not promised that it would be easy, were
we?

Too often we cut off responses to our inner rhythms because someone reprimands us with, "Be practical," or, "Who
do you think you are anyway, behaving in such a way . . . ?"

At one time or another we have all had sudden experiences
of "knowing" without any good reason, for there are times
when our mysterious subconscious does not depend on logic,
it just "knows that it knows." Never should our major decisions of what to do and how to do it be based solely on the
laws of logic and practicality without taking the promptings
of intuition, instinct, and inner feeling into consideration.

On the other hand, we should never allow fears without
foundation to keep us from pursuing that which we know is
right.

The Bible offers us hope against fear, the Psalms especially.

In the Twenty-seventh Psalm, the first verse, David exults,
*"The Lord is the strength of my life, of whom shall I be
afraid?"*

The Fifty-third Psalm, the fifth verse, tells us, *"There were
they in great fear where no fear was."*

"Where no fear was!" Fear so often is only the product of
our imaginations. There will be some who read this and say,
"Jeane Dixon is lucky! She could not mistake her gift of
prophecy. It came naturally . . . It is something so rare that
she doesn't have to be afraid."

Many of these people think of me as someone who lives on
a pink cloud without a care or worry in the world, gathering
fame and riches while foreseeing all sorts of world-shaking
events, but that is not the way it is at all. Money earned
through the use of my psychic gift goes to charity. My live-
lihood is earned in the real estate business in which I have
been actively engaged now for over twenty-five years.

Often friends ask, "Don't you ever take a vacation?" and stare at me when I explain to them that every working day is a vacation day for me. I love doing what God created me to do, also trying to help my fellow-men find out what God created them to do.

Parents who seemingly have not yet found out what they were created to do thus are out of harmony with themselves and the universe, so they complain constantly and bitterly about their jobs and their daily tasks, thus conditioning their children to look upon work as a necessary evil. Boys and girls who spend their formative years listening to complaining parents are all too likely to look upon their future positions and future employers the same way. And girls, subject to mothers who lament the thankless, monotonous drudgery of housework, have high hurdles of prejudice to overcome before, as adults, they recognize homemaking as a blessed privilege and can bring warmth and charm to their homes and take loving pride in caring for their families.

Not all of us have been given talents that will bring fame or riches. Some of us are called to work in areas of endeavor to which no worldly prestige is attached and where the remuneration is not above average. But we can, *working at our own talents in our own CHANNEL*, help others to achieve their purposes and so know the fulfillment of the spirit that comes to us when we truly live in our appointed ways.

In every office a staff of junior executives, secretaries, clerks, and others is needed to back up the man at the top without whom the entire operation would not exist. Staff salaries and responsibilities vary with the type of work done and the ratio of supply and demand. In a broader sense, there must be farmers and mechanics, teachers and salesmen, architects, builders, artists, and dreamers to provide food, build houses, construct machinery, teach the young, sell the products, and beautify our lives. Others fulfill their appointed jobs in government, publishing, or the creative arts, and again remuneration does not depend only on the type of work performed but also on the ratio of supply and demand, which in turn is closely related to the specific requirements of the particular industry and the ability of the individual.

Such is the pattern of the world in which we live, but status is not the measure of a full and fruitful life. Title and income do not equal purpose in life.

Let us never forget that while fame and riches do not preclude happiness or contentment, neither do they guarantee it. Nor can all the riches in the world buy those blessings.

A wealthy woman I know is, in my opinion, the poorest soul with whom I have ever come in contact. She has allowed her fortune to become an obsession to her and lives in constant fear of losing it. By placing more value on her money than is justified—afraid of being overcharged—she actually deprives herself of the necessities for her well-being. Sincere interest in her activities and health is regarded as useless flattery; she is convinced that her friends and relatives associate with her only because of her wealth. As a hypochondriac she is unsurpassed. It is the only thing she has to occupy her mind.

God has given her riches and time to spend on the poor and needy, yet she is unwilling to donate any time to the countless charitable organizations which rely on volunteer help and donations. She has many talents but flatly refuses to recognize or utilize them.

She is indeed a "lost soul"—and, ironically, poor because she is wealthy. . . .

Talents, however important, are not the only birth gifts given to us by God. We are also endowed with personality genes, some of which have the power to attract, others to rebuff. It is up to us, using our freedom of choice, to encourage or discourage these built-in tendencies as we develop our personalities. This determination of personality is never ending. Destructive characteristics which arise from time to time, especially under stress, have to be overcome. So do all impulses to imitate, for then we seek to pattern ourselves after someone else. However greatly we may admire another person, if we drift away from our own talents and our own channels we diminish the importance of our own personalities and the potential of our own individual gifts. *And to diminish that which we alone in the world possess is to reject the will of God,* and that is self-destructive.

There is only one of each of us. We are individual creations. The more faithfully we develop our talents and remain true to our given courses, the more we will be able to enjoy the harvests of the gifts of life.

We have in our office a valued associate, Iletha Herring. Until her twenty-second year she worked in my favorite beauty salon.

I first became aware of her because she was painstakingly particular about the little things she did. I could feel her vibrations as I watched her work. She worked as though it was a privilege, not a chore, and I felt her deep appreciation for the opportunity to earn an honorable living.

Many times when she was scolded unjustly in front of customers, she disciplined herself to smile and maintain her dignity, although others did not.

Noting the sincere devotion this beautiful Negro girl displayed toward her job, I asked her if she wanted to continue working as a hairdresser's helper.

She shook her head.

"No, not really," she answered, "but I'm afraid to try anything else. I know I can do this, and the money I make here is very important to my mother and me."

"Go to night school, learn typing and shorthand, and I will find you a place in our office," I promised. *Six months later, while still attending her evening classes, Iletha joined us as a clerk-typist.*

Every story has an ending and Iletha's is no exception. Her change in position gave her the confidence she needed and opened up the avenue for an entirely new life, for two summers ago she married the young lawyer, Hubert T. Jones, she had met a year previously.

"When I first met him," she recalled, "and found he was a lawyer, I wanted to run . . . I didn't want him to know about my job. Not that I felt the work I did was demeaning—to work is not degrading—but I wondered how he would feel about my being twenty-one years of age and not having more ambition in life. So I stopped seeing him."

Shortly after she joined us, however, Iletha renewed her acquaintance with Hubert.

Iletha has now found her true talents and is using them to begin to fulfill her destiny.

Today she is our head bookkeeper and the mother of a beautiful baby girl, Felicia Jeane, who is my godchild . . . bless her.

I have always believed that my true purpose for using my psychic talent is trying to help other people—not by "reading their futures," but by helping them to help themselves discover their own talents and to use them in their daily living for the glory of God. People who do learn to help themselves are the true "angels" of this world. For be they ever so meek, disadvantaged, impoverished, or seemingly deserted, if they try to help themselves they can stand straight, tall and proud, radiant . . . an example for all to see and follow.

One such remarkable and exemplary person is Mrs. Mary Walker of Chattanooga, Tennessee, affectionately called "Gramma" by all. Although born right after the termination of the Civil War, 103 years ago, truly a disadvantaged black child, she grew up with one fervent desire in life—to learn how to read.

When asked why, she replied, "To be able to study the Bible and learn more about God."

So, Gramma Walker, at the age of ninety-nine, enrolled in a reading class conducted by a social and civic group known as CALM.

"A very bright and talented student," her teacher said of

her following the first few sessions. "Amazing, considering her age . . ."

Take a moment to think about this fragile little lady, armed with an unwavering determination to advance herself, born into a period of reconstruction, reared among the prejudices of the times, seemingly without any chance in life. Yet she was filled with the love of God, and so Gramma Walker, almost a century old, enrolled in a reading course to find out more about her Creator. And yet how many much younger people hang their heads and say, "It's too late for me to change."

What greater courage could anyone display? No one knows for sure, but I, for one, would like to believe that God holds Gramma Walker among those closest to His heart!

Prayer and devotion—what do they mean? Contact between God and us can be made not only at recognized places of worship, for God in His infinity knows neither time nor limitations. Often I find myself praying for guidance and help while walking a busy way or crossing a crowded street, and there have been times when I felt His actual presence in answer to a prayer while being jostled by a crowd.

The biographers of Jenny Lind, the great singer, tell how she used to pray silently in her crowded dressing room and in the wings of the concert halls as she awaited her cue, amid the nervous activities of other members of the company.

Never questioning that her voice was a gift from God, she considered it her responsibility to use her talent well and to share the worldly riches it earned her with the needy.

Washington mornings at seven o'clock I enter St. Matthew's Cathedral, and when I am in prayer, nothing seems to distract me.

I have had great devotion to the Holy Mother ever since I was a child. Danny Thomas, on the other hand, has deep devotion and a habit of prayer to St. Jude, the patron saint of "impossible" things. He started this as a young man when he prayed for guidance and a particular job in show business.

He vowed that if he got the job, in gratitude he would build a hospital to St. Jude.

His prayer was answered! Danny Thomas got the job and St. Jude got his hospital! Danny built it in his honor in Tennessee, and today it stands for all the world to see, because he believed in prayer.

All this, by the way, does not mean that Catholics worship statues or believe that statues embody divine spirit. These beautiful representations of those who lived before us are meant to remind us of the saints' ways of life and of their good deeds and, hopefully, to inspire us to use our individual talents, privileges, and opportunities in much the same manner that the saints did, thereby fulfilling God's purpose for us as individuals.

Prayer is an act of the heart and soul. It is therefore not necessary to kneel as we pray. The Bible says nothing about kneeling as a prerequisite to prayer. Kneeling, it is believed, came about in the Middle Ages when it became the custom for serfs to kneel before the lord of the manor.

I like to kneel when I pray, for on my knees I feel more humble and reverent.

I feel closer to Him, too, when I seek Him in the quiet of the cathedral, for there is very little quiet in our modern world. We live with noise and dissonance from morning till night, and all, whether it be radio, television, stereo, or just conversation, call for our undivided attention. To commune with our Creator, therefore, we first must shut out that which tends to distract us from this privileged communication.

I have great admiration for the silent worship of the Quakers. The congregation, meditating in utter silence, waits to experience the workings of the Holy Spirit within them. Those who have experienced this blessed feeling tell me it blends the spiritual and the physical in complete harmony.

God is where we seek Him.

Remember—all churches are in the hands of God; God is not in the hands of any church.

Of the Bibles that are sent to me with requests to write a short message on the flyleaf, more come from Mormons than from any others.

Such interest in the Bible inspires me because it demonstrates that, however wide the difference in our forms of worship and religious concepts, we all look to the same spiritual source from whence comes everything in the universe, seen and unseen, heard and unheard.

In his book, *The Eighth Day*, Thornton Wilder tells us, "Religions are merely the garments of faith," and the truth in this statement is profound.

Spirituality in your daily life does not necessarily mean that your life will be all roses. Many people find it difficult to accept God as a loving Father image unless life is entirely to their liking. Any time their suffering is long or intense, they feel deserted by Him. They have somehow become convinced that because they have accepted God their years will be free from worry, pain, or any other unpleasantness. They accept God on their terms, not on His. They will not accept the fact that suffering, which is as inevitable in this creation as dawn, can be another one of God's ways to make them grow spiritually. To love God and our fellow-men when we are filled with sadness and pain is to love beautifully and truly.

There are those also who doubt any time a prayer seems to be unanswered. Our Lord answers our prayers in His way and in His time, not in ours. Do we not do the same with requests from our own children? Fulfillment of our desires may not always be in our best interests, so God, while hearing our prayers, does not shrug them aside but may say, "No, not this time," or, "No, not now."

There have been many instances in my life when His purpose for me has worked out beyond my fondest expectations, hopes, and dreams, but always in His time, not mine.

This can also apply to every individual.

Others, those of little faith—and sometimes of great arrogance—demand to know why God, "if He is a merciful Father," allows catastrophes like wars, floods, and earthquakes to occur. It may very well be one of His ways to demonstrate that there is indeed a power greater than ours. Only God knows why He permits a catastrophe. But He has His reasons. "God moves in a mysterious way His wonders to perform."

When John F. Kennedy, youthful and vibrant, was killed at the very time he sought to win the trust and understanding of the peoples of the world, the plaintive cry of "Why . . . ? Why . . . ?" was heard round the world. It is possible that John Fitzgerald Kennedy became President of the United States and internationally admired and loved so that he might come to his martyrdom—God's purpose for him, if not his own. Our human plans are not always in accord with God's plan. God alone is great enough to bring continuing good out of what may at times appear to be tragic and evil.

We may not visualize things God's way, yet it is certain that the will which ultimately prevails is

Not the will of the individual . . .
Not the will of the minority . . .
Not the will of the majority . . .
Not the will of the consensus . . .
Not the will of politicians and heads of state . . .
Or the will of nations,
But the will of God!

Therefore, as we orbit the earth, launch satellites, descend into the ocean's depths, and attempt to re-create life itself in the laboratory, let us always remember that it is God who gave us the talents and the abilities to accomplish these things.

There was a time, not so very long ago, when scientific findings were thought to be in disharmony with religion. Today the opposite is true. Yet we will not find faith through science. Although science continually uncovers the wonders of His creation, faith must ultimately come from within. However, as we tap into the mainstream of knowledge in the universe and become initiated in the mysteries of God, He provides us with the opportunity to become increasingly and reverently aware that we have our own purposes in life which must be fulfilled in order for us to be in harmony with the law of the universe.

Every morning we awaken to a reality—the reality that a new day of life has been granted us to employ as we please. How rich and rewarding this day becomes and how much we can accomplish depend entirely on us.

If we choose to approach it with depression and displeasure, if we are reluctant to probe into the possibilities extended to us and utilize the new day to its fullest potential, then we will have removed ourselves one day further away from our Creator.

If, however, we reach out with eagerness and love and cherish every God-given opportunity of every day, then we will feel as though we are in the company of angels.

Each day is a new creation that begins when the long, slender fingers of the morning sun pierce the path of the retreating moon and gather color from the eternal skies in order to create that spell of blushing light we call sunrise.

I try continuously, without ever really succeeding, to understand those who stand spellbound before a painting of a sunrise yet will not get up in time to witness its beauty in reality.

For me sunrise and worship go hand in hand. One of the pleasures of my life is to stand at my bedroom window in the early morning and recite the Twenty-third Psalm while observing the sun's radiant burst.

> "The Lord is my shepherd; I shall not want,
> He maketh me to lie down in green pastures;
> He leadeth me beside the still waters.
> He restoreth my soul.
> He leadeth me in the paths of righteousness for His
>   name's sake;

Yea, though I walk through the valley of the shadow of
death
I will fear no evil.
Thy rod and thy staff they comfort me.
Thou preparest a table before me in the presence of mine
enemies;
Thou anointest my head with oil; my cup runneth over.
Surely goodness and mercy shall follow me all the days of
my life,
And I shall dwell in the house of the Lord forever."

Every sunrise is an indescribable experience. No two clouds
are ever alike, and the streaming rays of the morning sun
never repeat their patterns. A sunrise is an ever-changing
kaleidoscope of beauty, an ever-changing miracle greater than
all telling.

When we see that flaming sphere break the horizon, we not
only become a witness to God's handiwork, we also add conscious hours to our day.

Three hundred and sixty-five times a year life offers
another opportunity to increase the value of our existence
and opens the door to a new level of fulfillment and accomplishments. It presents a chance to see and listen, to make
new friends, share our blessings anew, and become less criti-
cal and more tolerant toward our fellow-men.

It takes more than just a little patience and application of
our inner selves to train ourselves to see with our hearts as
well as our eyes and to listen with our minds as well as our
ears. But the spiritual growth we experience is so illuminating it soon becomes an integral part of us. Friendship and
love are ours when our thoughts, words, and deeds are sincere and when understanding and good will replace resent-
ment and envy.

Many of the questions often asked me deal with the existence of God. Surely, most people believe in God, but not
all comprehend that God is the controlling factor behind
everything. God is in control every day, everywhere. God

is omnipotent—goodness and kindness personified—and above all, He is perfect love!

Today, however, a powerful wind of false doctrine is blowing among men. It seduces them toward a false concept of God.

"God does not exist," they say. "Not yet, anyway. He is coming into existence through evolution of this developing world.

"Man's civilized progress and growth," they continue, "is progress toward the divine." H. G. Wells, one of the advocates of this theory, holds that "men will be like Gods"—that "God" is the future, fully developed state of mankind on this planet.

Many people with whom I come in contact have been affected by this false belief. It has saturated them and, like poison gas, it spreads and suffocates those who partake of it.

It has been said, "The Creator has been banished from city and country life, from laws, art and morals." Yet I believe the most important thing in life is to *know* God and to have the right understanding of Him. For only when we understand Him and His aims for us can we come to realize that each one of us has a particular place and purpose in life. We came from God, and we will return to God. He would not be all-loving and all-merciful if He had not given us the means at the time of our creation to return to Him.

The talents with which we are born are the means of fulfilling our mission here on earth. But they were intended not only to enrich our own lives but to help others!

Of course, most people believe in God, even though their way of worshiping Him may be different. When Jesus Christ taught His followers the "Our Father," He was restoring the original concept of mankind, for it is just such an idea of God that the fathers and mothers of families in simple tribal societies teach their children. To them He may be Manitou, or the Great Spirit, or the Heavenly Father. The simpler the people, the closer to nature they are, and the more primitive is their life and faith.

The most important thing I have discovered in my own life is to have the right attitude toward God. Only when *you* have discovered, as I feel I have discovered, the right attitude will you make your own particular contribution to this world and fulfill your purpose for being.

How do you accomplish this?

By acquiring the habits and practice of prayer and meditation, discussed previously in this same chapter; through prayer we realize God is a Spirit, not a thing or a lifeless force. Prayer, it has often been said, is the life of the soul. Through it we can cultivate the sense of the sacredness and goodness of God, whether in our private and personal prayer or in public prayer together with others in our churches and temples.

Someone asked me once how to acquire the habit of prayer. It is simple—oh, so simple! It only takes two things: think about your life and your purpose; and consult the Bible to discover God and His revealed plan for this world. Through the Bible all of us can learn who God really is and that He is infinite. And with such a guide we are led toward prayer.

Two things you will soon learn as you study: the only way He can be reached is through the faith of the inner intelligence; and He can be found everywhere.

The primitive people and the nature tribes had a strong awareness of God's presence, and they had special places where they considered Him to dwell more particularly, even when they knew that He was everywhere and was to be found within the heart. Their sacred groves, sacred mountains, sacred places, and sacred times—all these things men everywhere have known and have cherished.

So, too, the Jews and the Christians.

"Go where thou wilt, the Lord's eye is watching; good nor evil escapes His scrutiny," it says in Proverbs 15:3.

For a real understanding of God, study His Word; for a

better understanding of yourself and your role upon this earth, pray for His guidance. Prayer does not oppose the designs of Providence and does not seek to alter them, but actually cooperates in the divine governance, for when we pray we begin to seek what God wills for us.

With this living faith in our loving God each one of us can find a oneness with Him—which is atonement. With this life of prayer and daily work, developing as fully as we can the gifts He has given us, each of us is brought into harmony with His will.

12

Reincarnation

"Is there such a thing as reincarnation?"

"Do you believe in reincarnation?"

These are two of the questions most frequently asked me. Why does this subject intrigue people so? Because it grips them with something inflexibly true about God, about human history, and about the spark of life in each human being.

Even in its false form, reincarnation is a groping . . . a search to find the continuity of God's purposes in human life and in human history. In its true form it recognizes God as the Lord of universal history, but also as the Lord of each human, personal history. God is the Lord of the tapestry called "world history"—a tapestry woven out of all the personal histories of each and every one of us, drawn together.

What does the word reincarnation mean? "Incarnation" stems from the Latin "in-carne," meaning "to be in the flesh." And of course the prefix "re" means simply "again," as in "return," or "reinvigorate." "Reincarnation," therefore, means "to be in the flesh—again."

Christ, our Lord, was the Divine Word made flesh, dwelling with us on this earth in the flesh. Therefore we Christians speak of His "Incarnation" and say that Jesus Christ is "God Incarnate" (in the flesh).

Reincarnation is the belief that a man can be, or actually has been, incarnate more than once.

It is a common precept among those who believe in reincarnation that a human soul, which makes one the living individual that he is, has dwelled, dwells now, or is to dwell in other human bodies. Furthermore, in some forms of the doctrine, there is a belief that one and the same human soul is "incarnated" and "reincarnated" in different kinds of animals. This, of course, is very degrading to the human spirit and is, therefore, thought to be a punishment for failing to live up to the right standard of conduct for a human being.

As a result, sometimes it is taught that "reincarnation" in a lower form of animal is the greatest kind of punishment. It is surprising and regrettable how widespread these forms of the doctrine are among men!

People often tell me they are sure they were incarnated before in a different body because they seem to remember so distinctly that they have seen certain things before, or met certain persons or situations before. But when these instances are analyzed, especially by the medical men professionally competent to do so, it turns out that they are the results of their own imaginations.

Even Plato, the ancient philosopher, believed that the human soul had a pre-existence in heaven and the realm of divine ideas before it came to this earth for its term of imprisonment—or incarnation—in a body. Plato thought that the most noble aspect of human knowledge—its awareness of fundamental principles of goodness, truth, beauty, right and wrong, were explained by what the soul learned among the divine ideas in its pre-existence.

Yet modern psychologists prove conclusively what Aristotle and Saint Thomas Aquinas taught, that all our knowledge is based upon and derived from our sensory experiences after our birth into this earthly life. There is no aspect of human knowledge that depends upon a previous incarnation or previous existence.

Each of us is free to accept or reject individual creeds. I reject all of the crude forms of this doctrine of reincarnation, the idea that the same human identity is "in the flesh" many times, even in that of lower animals. And yet—as in all things human—this false doctrine is a stumbling and a groping toward a truth. What is this truth? It concerns the continuity of God's purposes for us as individual human beings, which provides a continuity in the very flow of human history.

The clearest example of this occurs in the bond between the Old and the New Testaments of the Holy Bible. It was stated clearly by the Lord our God, speaking His Word in the Bible, that Elijah would come again to prepare the way for the Messiah. Asked about this, Christ told His disciples that Elijah had come in the person of John the Baptist. John was fulfilling in his day a mission and purpose in the spirit of Elijah—that is, preparing the way for the Incarnate Lord.

Because God is all-great and all-powerful, there is a "reincarnation" of purposes and missions, assigned to individuals in particular times and places, which gives continuity to the flow of God's plan in the history of men. What a magnificent concept!

When Christ said, *"Elijah has already come but they did not recognize him,"* he indicated that the spirit of Elijah was accomplishing a mission in the person of John the Baptist (Matthew 17:11-13). He was teaching us that John the Baptist had a particular purpose assigned to him by Almighty God —a continuation and fulfillment of the purpose which the prophet Elijah carried out in a manner *proper to his time* in the unfolding of God's plan.

Human history is a tapestry woven by Almighty God, and the threads He uses are the personal lives of each one of us —and each one of us has a mission to accomplish! And this mission is the continuation or the fulfillment of a specific mission that earlier souls were given to carry on in their earlier times. There is a sense of timing in the pattern woven into the tapestry. God assigns His purposes, His callings, His functions to each and every newly created soul, in such a way that a wonderful continuity is preserved between the missions and purposes and callings of earlier souls and of those who come later.

Scientists and scholars in these matters tell us there are two kinds of heritage among men—the biological heritage that we receive from our parents and ancestors by physical generation, and the cultural heritage that can come to us only by learning.

There is a third heritage, however, which gives perspective and purpose to the other two, and that is the continuing participation of Almighty God in the affairs of men. It is the heritage that can be perceived in the pattern of human history designed by the Divine Weaver. In that pattern we learn our heritage. From that pattern we inherit our spiritual values.

The continuity of these spiritual values is carried across the centuries by the particular missions and purposes that He assigns to individuals in their own times. By being faithful to this mission and purpose which God gives to each one of us, we maintain the continuity of the divine heritage of spiritual values.

Each one of us has—there is no doubt about it—a particular purpose and mission assigned by God that is a continuation of a purpose and mission which had been assigned to an earlier soul in an earlier time. In this way the Divine Weaver weaves His tapestry of universal history. In this way His Divine Plan flows on as one great continuous stream of assignments of purposes to each individual human being in his particular time—whether that time was long ago, now, or still to come.

This is God's law in conducting the universal history of mankind. This is the harmony which He weaves into His universe. This is the unbroken chain of continuity in human affairs, in the continuity of the great spiritual values and missions.

Our spiritual heritage is carried on as a seamless robe across the ages because of the assignment of purposes, "incarnated" through individual to individual, bequeathing the treasure so that human history moves from the past through the present into the future.

It is in this way that individual human souls in the present experience the sense of heritage with individuals in the past. Within their souls there is a "reincarnation" of the spirit of a mission and purpose begun long ago and to be carried on by them.

When a child is born—whether in a slum and destitute, or in a palace and of royal birth—it lives because the Lord has breathed the breath of life into it. The Lord our God has created another individual soul in that baby. He does so because He has an individual purpose for that baby—to carry on an assignment in this living, continuous stream of human history, to bring to fulfillment an assignment which other souls in earlier times had begun. Just as the spirit of Elijah reappeared and was fulfilled in that later individual, John the Baptist. The *spirit* of Elijah, not the *soul* of Elijah, was reincarnated in the person and the mission of John the Baptist. A soul is never reincarnated in another body, but the spirit of a mission unfulfilled is reincarnated until that purpose is completed.

Almighty God, the Lord of History, is our Divine Trinity —the one God in Three Persons, whom we Christians know by the light of our faith—Almighty God is the Father, and the Son, and the Holy Spirit. It is through Him, and through faith in Him—the faith taught by God, the Son Incarnate— that we become aware of the fact that each one of us has a purpose and mission; by our awareness we recognize that purpose; by recognizing it through faith we should work diligently to fulfill it; and with faith, by sincerely attempting to fulfill His purpose for us, we will reap rewards greater than all telling, beyond our fondest dreams.

I cannot say too often that each personal history is a thread in the tapestry that God is weaving. Each stitch, each small personal thread, is important, with a special and individual importance, in God's pattern for this tapestry.

In breathing our souls into our bodies, He gave each one of us some assignment, some mission, something to do in furthering His kingdom on earth.

The individual purpose each one of us has, however humble and modest, is supremely important, because no one else can accomplish it in just the same way; no one else has exactly the same gifts—the means to do it—in just the same manner or kind. Each one of us has particular gifts—the particular means—to fulfill his own particular purpose, and it is given to each one of us at precisely the right time. For the "right time," under God's Almighty power, and the timing of the purpose assigned to each person, is the clearest witness to His infinite greatness and power!

Furthermore, God's assignment of roles and functions to each of us takes place within the rising curve of human progress. Each person's purpose, when fulfilled in accordance with the Divine Plan, contributes at a precise moment of time to that human progress. Thus, at this very moment, great scientists work out their formulas and their discoveries under God's great timing; each has his scientific role and purpose to perform during his moment on the stage of human development.

It is all a part of God's Divine Plan for the universe that, in the development of mankind, the space age should have come now and not at the same time that Benjamin Franklin was discovering electricity in lightning from space through a key on his kite!

In other words, God has a purpose and function for each soul He creates, according to the timing of the work which that soul is called to do for some role, great or small, in human progress. Each one of us can cooperate in this advancing and rising human curve, by learning to recognize the purpose that God has assigned to each one of us, and by working to accomplish it through our own initiative, but always with His Divine Guidance.

Outer space, for example, belongs to God our Lord. As

these words were being written, three astronauts, Colonel Thomas P. Stafford, Commander Eugene A. Cernan, and Commander John W. Young, were orbiting the moon and aiding in a planned moon landing. The Houston *Post* asked me to meditate on these three men, their talents and purposes. With the talent the Lord has given me, I could see that the individual talents of each of these astronauts were as different as day and night—Stafford, the man of balance, with talent to guide and hold things on an even keel; Cernan, the man of adventure, with love and talent for new things; Young, the man of science, with the talent to analyze and invent and discover.

What a reflection of the Divine Trinity! Three men, with roles so different, yet linked together into a wonderfully unified team! And the role of each one was indispensable to the success of their moon shot. If one man had failed, the lives of all three might have been lost, and the flight certainly would have failed.

But with all three functioning—according to each one's individual mission, his purpose, his timing—as one unit, that flight around the moon succeeded.

The astronauts are a living example of this assignment of roles and purposes to everyone. God Himself does it in His providence over men and history. But if we do not all carry out the role assigned, as members of an appointed "team," if we fail in our personal missions or waste our existences trying to play a role that belongs to someone else, we gradually upset our unity and our teamwork, and then the flight of our planet, earth, begins to fail, causing frustrations, individual unrest, individual unhappiness, broken marriages, broken homes, and broken lives. And from the sum of many lives being led apart from God's purpose comes the turmoil and destruction of riots, revolutions, and wars among nations.

However, all this turmoil and strife can be stopped when, and *only* when, we begin to function as a team, with each one of us fulfilling his important purpose—however small it may seem to be in the eyes of men—in this our mission planned by the Almighty God.

My entire message is to call attention to the personal purposes, those divinely assigned purposes, that make all of us a great team—a team that can and should work together. Just as those astronauts were an important part of the NASA team working together in the conquest of space—a conquest which will be carried on by others—so, too, is each one of us an important part of God's work which will be carried on by others till the end of time.

And as the saints and holy writers tell us through the ages, God never fails with His help. When we recognize our personal purpose and begin to work it out as a member of His team—a worker in His vineyard—with all nations at peace, with each family united in a bond of love, with each individual free to develop his individual talents and to live a fruitful life in a healthy society, and with all faiths united under one God, such a world will come to pass.

When that time comes—and it will come—we will all be united in the Brotherhood of Christ under the Fatherhood of God.

When that time comes—and it will come—the Lord's prayer will be fully answered:

> "Our Father
> Who art in heaven,
> Hallowed be thy name.
> Thy kingdom come.
> Thy will be done on earth,
> As it is in heaven . . ."